☆ THINK YOU ☆
KNOW IT ALL?

DAN SMITH

THINK YOU KNOW IT ALL?

THE ACTIVITY BOOK
FOR GROWN-UPS

First published in Great Britain in 2010 by
Michael O'Mara Books Limited
9 Lion Yard
Tremadoc Road
London SW4 7NQ

A CIP catalogue record for this book is available from the
British Library.

Papers used by Michael O'Mara Books Limited are natural,
recyclable products made from wood grown in sustainable forests.
The manufacturing processes conform to the environmental
regulations of the country of origin.

ISBN: 978-1-84317-457-8

10

www.mombooks.com

Illustrations by David Woodroffe
Cover design by Allan Sommerville
Designed and typeset by Allan Sommerville
Printed and bound by CPI Group (UK) Ltd, Croydon, CR0 4YY

for Will & Helena

ACKNOWLEDGEMENTS

It is only fair to admit that these quizzes did not spring organically from a bottomless well of my own knowledge. If only… Instead, I have had great fun and learned a tremendous amount in the process of putting this collection together. I have been most ably assisted by a network of friends and loved ones who have contributed countless ideas for fun and testing questions. Many appear within these pages, while many other excellent ones have had to be excluded simply for lack of space. Thanks in particular to Anna Marx at Michael O'Mara for her guidance. And a special thanks, as ever, to Rosie, who I hope will always keep my feet on the ground should I erroneously get to thinking I know it all already.

INTRODUCTION

Nobody likes a know-it-all, do they? But if truth be told, most of us would gladly put up with the odd jibe if we could only be that know-it-all. This is, I hope, the perfect book to test your knowledge to the limit. Should you pass all the tests, you may award yourself the official title of Chief of the Smarty-Pants (before setting your mind to answering the question of the meaning of life, which should prove quite a doddle after all the brain-teasers contained herein).

Most quiz books set out to examine only the breadth of your knowledge. This one looks at the depth of your knowledge, too. Having a little knowledge about a lot or knowing a few trivia 'golden nuggets' just won't do. Rather, we will prod and probe to find out if you know any given subject inside out.

Where others might ask who was the first (or at a push, the second) man to walk on the Moon, this is the book that will ask you for the names of every human who has ever stepped foot on it. Or, if space travel is not your thing, what about the titles of every play that Shakespeare wrote? The bones of the human body? The member states of the EU? The cast of *Friends*? The plagues of Egypt?

From high culture to low, science, language, history, religion, transport, sport – I hope there are quizzes here that will appeal to every member of the family. Please don't expect to know the answers to everything straight away. Instead, pick a quiz that takes your fancy and give it time. Perhaps the greatest pleasure of all is to be gained by digging out the final answer to a quiz three days after you started it. Be sure to enjoy that slow-burning satisfaction!

And when you come across a quiz that leaves you completely stumped (there is no inherent shame in not being able to name the original crew of the USS *Enterprise* or all the Secretary Generals of the United Nations) simply look up the answers and then, when the opportunity arises, show off your new-found knowledge like you had known it all along.

A final bit of advice for when you have mastered these quizzes and do, indeed, know absolutely everything about everything. Always remember that the greatest fun to be had by a true know-it-all is not by boasting or bragging (such smugness will rightfully inspire scorn) but to set your knowledge valve to slow-release and look on as those around you discover for themselves just how clever you really are!

SO ... THINK YOU KNOW IT ALL?

The Solar System

Our solar system contains the Sun and, traditionally, nine planets (although one you probably remember from schooldays has now been downgraded to a 'dwarf planet'). Can you remember the names of all the planets (including the controversial ninth) in order of proximity to the sun?

1

2

3

4

5

6

7

8

9

☆ *Answers on page 160*

Name That Bird

Below are pictures of twenty types of bird found in various corners of the world. How many can you identify?

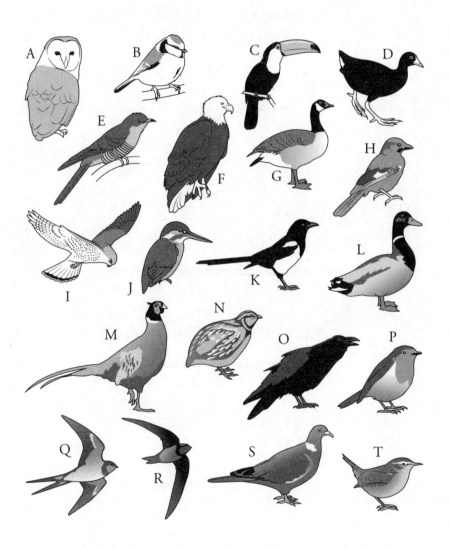

☆ *Answers on page 160*

Cube Numbers

A cube number is a number to its third power.
That is to say, $n^3 = n \times n \times n$ (where n = your original number).
Can you work out the cube of the numbers 1 to 15?
Definitely no calculators allowed!

Famous First Lines

Below are the first lines of ten classic novels.
Can you name the title and author of each?

*'1801 – I have just returned from a visit to my landlord – the solitary
neighbour that I shall be troubled with.'*

*'Mr Sherlock Holmes, who was usually very late in the mornings,
save upon those not infrequent occasions when he stayed up all night,
was seated at the breakfast table.'*

☆ *Answers on pages 160–1*

*'Among other public buildings in a certain town, which for many reasons
it will be prudent to refrain from mentioning, and to which I will assign
no fictitious name, there is one anciently common to most towns, great or
small: to wit, a workhouse; and in this workhouse was born; on a day and
date which I need not trouble myself to repeat, inasmuch as it can be of no
possible consequence to the reader, in this stage of the business at all events;
the item of mortality whose name is prefixed to the head of this chapter.'*

'I was born in the city of Bombay … once upon a time.'

*'The play – for which Briony had designed the posters, programmes and
tickets, constructed the sales booth out of a folding screen tipped on its side,
and lined the collection box with crêpe paper – was written by her
in a two-day tempest of composition, causing her to miss a breakfast
and a lunch.'*

*'"They made a silly mistake, though," the professor of history said, and his
smile, as Dixon watched, gradually sank beneath the surface of his features
at the memory.'*

*'Far out in the uncharted backwaters of the unfashionable end of the
western spiral arm of the Galaxy lies a small, unregarded yellow sun.'*

*'In my younger and more vulnerable years my father gave me some advice
I've been turning over in my mind ever since.'*

*'"Christmas won't be Christmas without any presents," grumbled Jo,
lying on the rug.'*

'Mother died today.'

☆ *Answers on pages 160–1*

The Phonetic Alphabet

The NATO Phonetic Alphabet is the most widely used phonetic alphabet in the world today. It is the one that starts 'Alpha, Bravo...' But how does it continue?

A		N	
B		O	
C		P	
D		Q	
E		R	
F		S	
G		T	
H		U	
I		V	
J		W	
K		X	
L		Y	
M		Z	

☆ The Harry Potter Novels ☆

J. K. Rowling has written seven novels in the Harry Potter series. Can you remember them in the order in which they were published?

☆ Answers on page 161

Tying Yourself in Knots

Most of us just about master tying our shoelaces, but how many of these basic knots can you recognize and name?

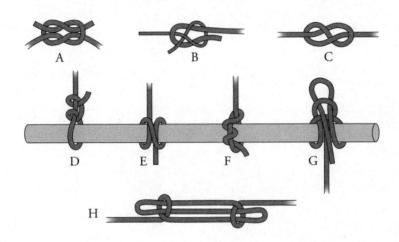

The Soccer World Cup

Seven different countries won the eighteen Soccer World Cups held up to 2006. Listed below are the numbers of victories each winner has had. Can you complete the list by working out which country fits where, and which years they triumphed at the tournament?

VICTORIES	TEAM	YEAR(S)
5		
4		
3		
2		
2		
1		
1		

☆ Answers on page 162

The European Union

As of 2010, the European Union comprised twenty-seven
member states. Can you list them all in alphabetical order,
along with their national capitals?

1

2

3

4

5

6

7

8

9

10

11

12

13

14

15

16

17

18

19

20

21

22

23

24

25

26

27

☆ *Answers on page 162*

The Books of the Old Testament

There are thirty-nine books in the 1611 King James Bible version of the Old Testament. What are their names in the order in which they appear?

✩ *Answers on page 163*

What's in a (City) Name?

Many cities have undergone name changes in their histories, whether as the result of conquest, the evolution of language or as a political statement. Below are listed the previous names of fifteen major world towns and cities. Can you identify them?

1   **Peking**

2   **Madras**

3   **Kingstown**

4   **Lyallpur**

5   **Danzig**

6   **Salisbury**

7   **Saigon**

8   **Constantinople**

9   **Leopoldville**

10 **New Amsterdam**

11 **Kristiania**

12 **Hanseong**

13 **Leningrad**

14 **Edo**

15 **Rangoon**

☆ Answers on page 163

Colours of the Rainbow

There are seven spectrums of colour in the rainbow.
What are they?

Fictional Crime-Fighting Sidekicks

Below are the names of eleven of the world's best-known
crime-fighters. But who were their erstwhile companions,
and can you remember their creators too?

1 **Batman**
2 **Elijah Baley**
3 **Tommy Beresford**
4 **D. Supt. Andy Dalziel**
5 **Sherlock Holmes**
6 **D. Insp. Tommy Lynley**
7 **Inspector Morse**
8 **Hercule Poirot**
9 **Chief Insp. Reg Wexford**
10 **Nero Wolfe**
11 **Insp. Roderick Alleyn**

Answers on page 164

International Airlines

Here are the logos of twenty international airlines.
All you have to do is name the company.

☆ *Answers on page 164*

Great Composers

How well do you know your classical music? Here are the dates of fifteen of the finest composers the world has ever seen, along with the names of some of their most famous works. Who are the composers?

1756–1791	*Eine kleine Nachtmusik*
1873–1943	*Rhapsody on a Theme of Paganini*
1840–1893	*The Nutcracker Suite*
1770–1827	*Moonlight Sonata*
1732–1809	*Surprise Symphony*
1833–1897	*Liebeslieder Waltzes*
1685–1750	*The Brandenburg Concertos*
1865–1957	*Finlandia*
1685–1759	*Messiah*
1810–1849	*The Minute Waltz*
1797–1828	*The Trout*
1811–1886	*Hungarian Rhapsodies*
1809–1847	*Hebrides Overture*
1676–1741	*The Four Seasons*
1841–1904	*Carnival Overture*

All the Vowels

There are a handful of English words that contain all of the five vowels in the correct order (a, e, i, o and u). How many can you get? A big pat on the back if you manage more than two!

✩ *Answers on pages 164–5*

The Eurovision Song Contest

Here are some of the most famous songs to have won the much-maligned Eurovision Song Contest. All you have to do is name the artist, the year they won and the country they represented.

SONG	ARTIST	YEAR	COUNTRY
'All Kinds Of Everything'			
'Boom Bang-A-Bang'			
'Diva'			
'Hard Rock Hallelujah'			
'Hold Me Now'			
'Love Shine A Light'			
'Making Your Mind Up'			
'Ne Partez Pas Sans Moi'			
'Puppet On A String'			
'Save Your Kisses For Me'			
'Waterloo'			
'What's Another Year'			

The Seven Wonders of the Ancient World

Of the Seven Wonders of the Ancient World, only one survives today. But what were the seven? And, for a bonus mark, which is still in existence?

☆ Answers on page 165

Metric and Imperial

It is broadly fair to say that the world is divided into two – those who have never got to grips with the metric system and those who can't think in any other terms. Here are a few classic Imperial measurements (of length, area, volume and weight). How many can you convert into metric (to two decimal places)?

IMPERIAL	METRIC
1 inch	cm
1 mile	km
1 hectare	m²
1 pint	litres
1 stone	kg
1 long ton	tonnes

The Symphony Orchestra

The modern Symphony Orchestra can be divided into four main parts: strings, woodwind, brass and percussion. Can you list all the instruments you might expect to find in each section?

STRINGS

WOODWIND

BRASS

PERCUSSION

✫ Answers on page 166

The James Bond Films

Star of one of the most successful movie franchises of all time,
Bond is the man all other men want to be and all women want
to be with. Just six lucky actors have had the chance to play him.
Below you have the actor and the year of each film – can you
recall the name of each movie?

SEAN CONNERY

1962

1963

1964

1965

1967

1971

1983

GEORGE LAZENBY

1969

ROGER MOORE

1973

1974

1977

1979

1981

1983

1985

☆ Answers on page 166

TIMOTHY DALTON

1987
1989

PIERCE BROSNAN

1995
1997
1999
2002

DANIEL CRAIG

2006
2008

Snooker Loopy

Snooker involves potting balls of different colours to earn points.
Can you remember which colour is worth how many points?

POINTS VALUE	COLOUR
1	
2	
3	
4	
5	
6	
7	

✩ *Answers on page 167*

International Currencies

Do you know your Real from your Dong? Below are the names
of various currencies. Can you name the country (or two countries)
in which each is used?

1 **Bolivar**

2 **Colón (2)**

3 **Dirham (2)**

4 **Dong**

5 **Forint**

6 **Hryvna**

7 **Koruna**

8 **Kwanza**

9 **Lek**

10 **Lilangeni**

11 **Naira**

12 **Ngultrum**

13 **Quetzal**

14 **Real**

15 **Ringgit**

16 **Ruble (2)**

17 **Sheqel**

18 **Yen**

19 **Yuan Renminbi**

20 **Zloty**

☆ *Answers on page 167*

Shakespeare's Plays

Traditionally, thirty-seven plays have been attributed to William Shakespeare, broadly grouped under the categories of Histories, Tragedies and Comedies. How many can you remember?

HISTORIES

TRAGEDIES

COMEDIES

☆ *Answers on pages 167–8*

The London Underground

The Circle Line on the London Underground takes in many of London's most famous areas. Here is a map of the original line. Starting at Paddington in the top left hand corner, can you fill in all the other station names?

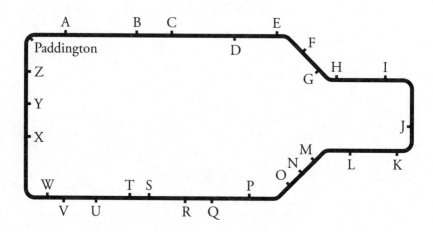

Snow White's Dwarfs

Can you remember the names of all seven dwarfs in Walt Disney's 1937 classic movie *Snow White and the Seven Dwarfs*?

☆ *Answers on pages 168–9*

Mixing it up

Think you know your booze? Well, here are the key ingredients of ten classic cocktails, as recognized by the International Bartenders' Association. Can you name them?

1 **Vodka, tomato juice, lemon juice**

2 **Gin, Heering cherry liqueur, Cointreau, Bénédictine liqueur, grenadine, pineapple juice, fresh lemon juice, Angostura Bitters**

3 **Vodka, tequila, white rum, triple sec, gin, lemon juice, gomme syrup, cola**

4 **White rum, lime juice, mint, sugar, soda water**

5 **Tequila, triple sec, lemon or lime juice**

6 **Vodka citron, triple sec, lime juice, cranberry juice**

7 **Vodka, Galliano, orange juice**

8 **Vodka, orange juice**

9 **Vodka, coffee liqueur, cream**

10 **Rye or Canadian whisky, sweet red vermouth, Angostura Bitters, maraschino cherry**

Answers on page 169

The Greek Alphabet

Our word 'alphabet' is derived from the names of the first two Greek letters, *alpha* and *beta*. The Greek alphabet consists of twenty-four letters in total. Below are the symbols for each. Can you give them their English names?

α β γ δ ε ζ η θ ι κ λ μ
i ii iii iv v vi vii viii ix x xi xii

ν ξ ο π ρ σ τ υ φ χ ψ ω
xiii xiv xv xvi xvii xviii xix xx xxi xxii xxiii xiv

Champagne Charlie

Champagne can come in a series of different-sized bottles. An ordinary bottle contains 75 cl. Do you know the names of the other sizes?

Standard bottle size equivalent

2

4

6

8

12

16

20

☆ *Answers on page 169*

US States and Their Capitals

Everyone knows that the capital of New York State is
New York City, don't they? Except it isn't. In this two-parter,
you need to identify each of the fifty states and their state capitals.
But, beware – it is often not the one you're expecting …

STATE	CAPITAL

✩ *Answers on page 170*

☆ Great Film Taglines ☆

Taglines are the slogans film marketeers come up with to reel us into the cinemas. Here are some of the most memorable in film history. With the additional clue of the year the film came out, can you match the tagline to the movie?

'*The strangest story ever conceived by man.*' (1933)

'*For anyone who has ever wished upon a star.*' (1940)

'*Dance she did, and dance she must – between her two loves.*' (1948)

'*What a Glorious Feeling!*' (1952)

'*Jim Stark – a kid from a "good" family – what makes him tick ... like a bomb?*' (1955)

'*Check in. Relax. Take a shower.*' (1960)

'*The Happiest Sound In All The World!*' (1965)

'*Being the adventures of a young man whose principal interests are rape, ultra-violence and Beethoven.*' (1971)

'*Don't go in the water.*' (1975)

'*On every street in every city, there's a nobody who dreams of being a somebody.*' (1976)

'*A long time ago, in a galaxy far, far away ...*' (1977)

☆ *Answers on pages 170–1*

'You'll Believe A Man Can Fly!' (1978)

'In space no one can hear you scream.' (1979)

'Who you gonna call?' (1984)

'He's the only kid ever to get into trouble before he was born.' (1985)

'The first casualty of war is innocence.' (1986)

'A tale of murder, lust, greed, revenge, and seafood.' (1988)

'Can two friends sleep together and still love each other in the morning?'
(1989)

'To enter the mind of a killer she must challenge the mind of a madman.'
(1991)

'He's having the worst day of his life ... over, and over ...' (1993)

'Fear can hold you prisoner. Hope can set you free.' (1994)

'A lot can happen in the middle of nowhere.' (1996)

'Reality is a thing of the past.' (1999)

'The greatest fairy tale never told.' (2001)

'Sometimes you have to go halfway around the world to come full circle.'
(2003)

⚖ *Answers on page 171*

World Landmarks

Here are twenty of the most famous sites around the world.
But do you know where each one is?

1   **Arch of Constantine**

2   **Heroes' Square**

3   **The World archipelago**

4   **Statue of Christ the Redeemer**

5   **Diocletian's Palace**

6   **Stari Most**

7   **Abu Simbel**

8   **CN Tower**

9   **Ruins of Machu Picchu**

10 **Saint Basil's Cathedral**

11 **The Forbidden City**

12 **Temple of the Golden Pavillion**

13 **Sagrada Família**

14 **Uluru**

15 **Mount Rushmore National Memorial**

16 **Taj Mahal**

17 **Blue Mosque**

18 **Little Mermaid Statue**

19 **Hofburg Imperial Palace**

20 **Acropolis**

☆ Answers on page 171

Types of Tree

Here are the leaves of twenty well-known types of trees.
How many can you identify?

✿ *Answers on pages 171–2*

The Signs of the Zodiac

There are twelve star signs, providing horoscope writers the world over with a never-ending source of material. But what are they?

Scrabble Tiles

In the game of Scrabble, each letter is worth a set amount of points. Can you complete the table below (the figure in parenthesis indicates the number of letters of that particular value)?

POINTS VALUE	LETTER(S)
1 point (10)	
2 points (2)	
3 points (4)	
4 points (5)	
5 points (1)	
8 points (2)	
10 points (2)	

The Oscars:
The Biggest Winners

As of 2009, twenty-five films had achieved a haul of seven or more Oscars. Can you name them? To give you a clue, the table below gives you the total number each film won and the year it won them.

NO. OF WINS	YEAR	FILM
11	1997	
11	1959	
11	2003	
10	1961	
9	1996	
9	1958	
9	1987	
8	1939	
8	1953	
8	1954	
8	1964	
8	1982	
8	1984	
8	1972	
8	2008	
7	1998	
7	1990	
7	1993	
7	1985	
7	1944	
7	1962	
7	1970	
7	1973	
7	1946	
7	1957	

☆ *Answers on page 172*

Great Artists

Below are the dates of twenty of the greatest artists of all time, along with the names of some of their most famous works. Can you name the artist in each case?

1869–1954	*The Conversation*
1606–69	*The Night Watch*
1881–1973	*Guernica*
1483–1520	*The School of Athens*
1839–1906	*The Card Players*
1863–1944	*The Scream*
1840–1926	*Impression, Sunrise*
1853–90	*The Potato Eaters*
1904–89	*The Persistence of Memory*
1452–1519	*The Last Supper*
1571–1610	*Boy With a Basket of Fruit*
1866–1944	*Yellow-red-blue*
1862–1918	*Adele Bloch-Bauer I*
1898–1967	*The Treachery of Images*
1928–87	*Campbell's Soup I*
1907–54	*Self Portrait With Thorn Necklace and Hummingbird*
1834–1917	*The Dance Class*
1841–1919	*Luncheon of the Boating Party*
1475–1564	*The Hand of God*
c.1490–1576	*Bacchus and Ariadne*

☆ *Answers on page 173*

Songs From the Musicals

We all like a show with some good tunes but sometimes the songs become more famous than the shows themselves. Can you remember which musical gave birth to these anthems?

'You'll Never Walk Alone'

'Oh, What A Beautiful Morning'

'There's No Business Like Show Business'

'Ol' Man River'

'Summertime'

'Luck Be A Lady'

'Hopelessly Devoted To You'

'Who Wants To Be A Millionaire? '

'Something Wonderful '

'Always True To You In My Fashion'

'Feed The Birds'

'On The Street Where You Live'

'As Long As He Needs Me'

'The Music Of The Night'

'La Vie Bohème'

'The Time Warp'

'Happy Talk'

'Sixteen Going On Seventeen'

'America'

'I Dreamed A Dream'

☆ *Answers on page 173*

The Human Skeleton

The average adult body hangs on a frame of 206 bones.
Can you label those identified on the diagram below?

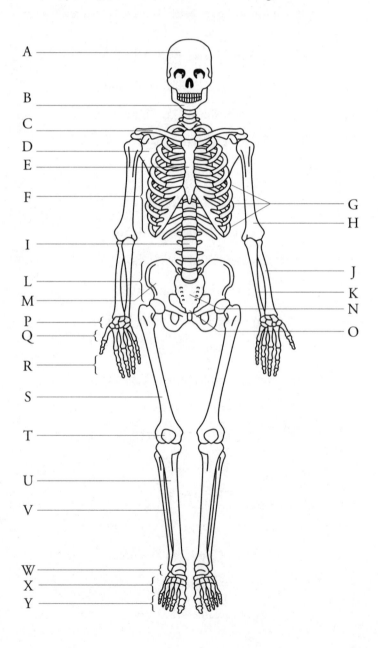

☆ *Answers on pages 173–4*

The Safari 'Big Five'

The test of a truly great safari is whether you manage to see examples of all the animal types that comprise the 'Big Five'. It was a list originally created by big game hunters on the basis of which animals were hardest to kill. Which species make up the classic 'Big Five'?

The Modern Decathlon

Which ten athletic events make up the decathlon?

The World's Longest Rivers

Below are the lengths of the eight longest rivers in the world. Can you work out which they are?

LENGTH (KM)	RIVER
6,695	
6,516	
6,380	
6,019	
5,570	
5,550	
5,464	
4,667	

☆ Answers on page 174

The Periodic Table

Here are a few testers to see how well you remember the dreaded
Periodic Table, which was invented by Dmitri Mendeleev in 1869.
To make it a bit easier, you're given the atomic number and the
chemical symbols that represent each element.

(A) To get you started, can you remember the first eight elements?

ATOMIC NUMBER	CHEMICAL SYMBOL	ELEMENT NAME
1	H	
2	He	
3	Li	
4	Be	
5	B	
6	C	
7	N	
8	O	

(B) What about the Noble gases?

ATOMIC NUMBER	CHEMICAL SYMBOL	ELEMENT NAME
2	He	
10	Ne	
18	Ar	
36	Kr	
54	Xe	
86	Rn	

☆ Answers on pages 174–5

(c) **And a few more random ones to finish off.**

ATOMIC NUMBER	CHEMICAL SYMBOL	ELEMENT NAME
11	Na	
12	Mg	
19	K	
22	Ti	
33	As	
45	Rh	
50	Sn	
74	W	
79	Au	
94	Pu	
104	Rf	

What the Romans Did for Us

We use plenty of Latin phrases in everyday speech, but do we always know exactly what they mean? Here are ten definitions. Which Latin phrase does each describe?

1 A great work.
2 A thing given in return for another.
3 A writ requiring a person to be brought before a judge.
4 For a particular purpose.
5 In the very act of committing an offence.
6 Let the buyer beware.
7 Within the glass.
8 The other way around.
9 The school, college or university one attends or attended.
10 The way in which an individual performs a task.

☆ *Answers on page 175*

Great Poems

Here are the famous first lines of fifteen poems.
What are the names of the poems and who wrote them?

'*'Twas brillig, and the slithy toves …*'

'*I met a traveller from an antique land …*'

'*Remember me when I am gone away …*'

'*How do I love thee? Let me count the ways.*'

'*Should auld acquaintance be forgot …*'

'*That Whitsun, I was late getting away …*'

'*What passing-bells for these who die as cattle?*'

'*Season of mists and mellow fruitfulness …*'

'*There's a whisper down the line at 11.39 …*'

'*Half a league, half a league …*'

'*If you can keep your head when all about you …*'

'*Stop all the clocks, cut off the telephone …*'

'*Once upon a midnight dreary, while I pondered weak and weary …*'

'*Earth has not anything to show more fair …*'

'*Shall I compare thee to a summer's day?*'

The Hits of Elvis

Elvis Presley had thirty-one tracks that made it to
the top of the charts in either the USA or the UK.
Can you recall them all?

✩ *Answers on page 176*

Noms de Plume

Throughout history, some of the greatest writers have hidden behind pseudonyms. Here are the real names of ten hugely successful wordsmiths. Can you work out which names they wrote under?

Anne Brontë

Theodor Seuss Geisel

Mary Ann Evans

Eric Arthur Blair

David John Moore Cornwell

Józef Teodor Nalecz Konrad Korzeniowski

Charles Lutwidge Dodgson

Samuel Langhorne Clemens

Thomas Lanier Williams

Tomas Straussler

☆ Answers on page 176

US Military Ranks

The US Army has twenty-nine recognized ranks, starting
with Private and ending with General of the Army.
But what are all the ones in between?

☆ *Answers on page 177*

Who's the Actor?

Eleven actors have taken the eponymous role of Dr Who. Can you remember them all? A bonus point for the name of the actor who played 'the first Doctor' in a 1983 special, *The Five Doctors*.

Great Inventions

Here is a list of inventions that have helped shape the world we live in today. But who were the great minds that created them?

Ball-point pen	**Mechanical calculator**
Clockwork radio	**Microwave oven**
Coca-Cola	**Phonograph**
Dynamite	**Printing press**
Frozen food	**Spinning Jenny**
Hot-air balloon	**Stethoscope**
Jet engine	**Telephone**
Machine gun	

Books of the
New Testament

In the King James Bible of 1611, there are
twenty-seven New Testament Books. What are they?

✩ *Answers on page 178*

Birthstones

For each month of the year there is an associated stone.
Can you name the twelve?

New Nations

Since the dissolution of the USSR into fifteen new nations in 1991,
a further twelve new countries (as recognized by the UN) have
come into existence around the world. Here are the dates of their
establishment. Can you name them?

1991

1991

1991

1991

1992

1992

1993

1993

1993

1993

1994

2002

☆ Answers on page 178

Famous Dates in History

Below are fifteen defining moments of human history.
In which years did they occur?

The Foundation of Rome

Birth of Buddha

**Constantine, the Roman Emperor,
converted to Christianity**

Birth of Muhammad

**Signing of the Magna Carta by
King John of England**

**Christopher Columbus made his discovery
of the New World**

Signing of the American Declaration of Independence

The French Revolution

Battle of Waterloo ended the Napoleonic Empire

Charles Darwin published *The Origin of Species*

Einstein published his theory of relativity

The Russian Revolution

The Second World War ended

The silicon chip was invented

Collapse of the Berlin Wall

✨ *Answers on page 179*

The Morse the Merrier

We all know that if you're in trouble and you need to communicate via Morse Code, trust in a simple ... - - - ... (S.O.S). How well do you know the rest of the alphabet, though?

A	J	S
B	K	T
C	L	U
D	M	V
E	N	W
F	O	X
G	P	Y
H	Q	Z
I	R	

Which Trophy, Which Sport?

Below are the names of ten coveted sports trophies. Can you work out which sport you'd need to play to be in with a chance of getting your hands on each one?

TROPHY	SPORT
William Webb Ellis Cup	
Stanley Cup	
America's Cup	
Larry O'Brien Trophy	
Vince Lombardi Trophy	
Fed Cup	
Walker Cup	
Yellow Jersey	
Breeders' Cup	
Thomas Cup	

☆ Answers on page 179

The Summer Olympics

The Modern Olympic Games were first held in 1896.
Can you match each year below to the host city?

YEAR	CITY
1896	
1900	
1904	
1908	
1912	
1920	
1924	
1928	
1932	
1936	
1948	
1952	
1956	
1960	
1964	
1968	
1972	
1976	
1980	
1984	
1988	
1992	
1996	
2000	
2004	
2008	
2012	
2016	

☆ Answers on page 180

French Wine Regions

Here is a map of France with the major wine regions indicated.
Can you identify them?

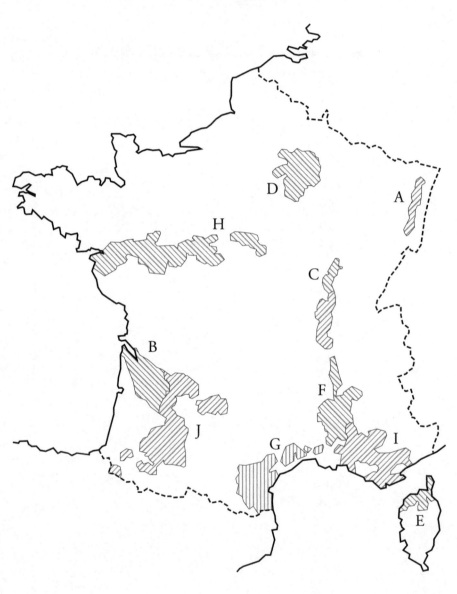

☆ *Answers on page 180*

Kings and Queens of England and Britain

When Charles I literally lost his head in 1649, England began eleven years of life without a monarch. But before long the institution was revived. Can you name all the kings and queens since 1660?

DATES	MONARCH
1660–85	
1685–88	
1688–1702	
1688–94	
1702–14	
1714–27	
1727–60	
1760–1820	
1820–30	
1830–37	
1837–1901	
1901–10	
1910–36	
1936	
1936–52	
1952–	

✧ *Answers on pages 180–1*

The World's Highest Mountains

Do you know the names of the highest mountains on each continent?

CONTINENT	HEIGHT (METRES)	MOUNTAIN
Asia	8,850	
South America	6,960	
North America	6,194	
Africa	5,900	
Europe	5,633	
Antarctica	4,987	
Australasia	2,230	

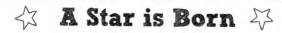

☆ A Star is Born ☆

Some of the most famous names in entertainment swapped the names they were born with for something a little more glitzy. Here are the birth names of twenty-five major stars. How are they better known?

Marvin Lee Aday

Frederick Austerlitz

William Bailey

Norma Jeane Baker

Anna Mae Bullock

Reginald Dwight

Eileen Regina Edwards

Ernest Evans

Vincent Furnier

Frances Gumm

Virginia Patterson Hensley

☆ Answers on page 181

Paul Hewson
Caryn Johnson
Steveland Judkins
Allen Konigsberg
Cherilyn Sarkisian
Archibald Leach
Marion Morrison
Georgios Krylacos Panayiotou
Betty Joan Perske
Bernard Schwartz
Gordon Sumner
Brian Warner
Julia Wells
Robert Zimmerman

Best Actor Oscars

Nine men have won the Best Actor Academy Award twice. Can you work out who they are just from the years that they won?

YEARS	ACTOR
1931/32, 1946	
1937, 1938	
1941, 1952	
1954, 1972	
1975, 1997	
1979, 1988	
1989, 2007	
1993, 1994	
2003, 2008	

☆ *Answers on page 181*

Best Actress Oscars

As for the women, one lady is ahead of the pack with four wins, and seven others have won twice. Again, here are the years but what are the names?

YEARS	ACTRESS
1932-33, 1967, 1968, 1981	
1935, 1938	
1936, 1937	
1939, 1951	
1944, 1956	
1946, 1949	
1960, 1966	
1970, 1973	
1971, 1978	
1979, 1984	
1988, 1991	
1999, 2004	

 # How Many Players?

Below is a selection of popular team sports. How many in-game players do you need for a team in each sport?

Soccer
Rugby Union
Rugby League
Field Hockey
Ice Hockey
Polo

☆ *Answers on pages 181–2*

Basketball
Baseball
American Football
Cricket
Aussie Rules
Lacrosse (Men)
Lacrosse (Women)

International Organizations Acronyms

Many international organizations are known best by their acronyms. Can you give the full names of the organizations listed below?

EFTA
FAO
IAEA
IBRD (The World Bank)
ICRC
IMF
IOC
NATO
OECD
OPEC
UN
UNESCO
WHO
WIPO
WTO

⭐ *Answers on page 182*

The Chronicles of Narnia

C. S. Lewis documented the history of the imaginary land of Narnia in seven books of enduring popularity. You have the year of publication of each to start you off, but can you name them all?

YEAR	TITLE
1950	
1951	
1952	
1953	
1954	
1955	
1956	

Animal Collective Nouns

The English language is rarely livelier than when describing groups of particular animals. Here are fifteen collective nouns that are particularly rich in imagery. To which species does each refer?

1 **Cackle**
2 **Charm**
3 **Colony**
4 **Intrusion**
5 **Knot**
6 **Labour**
7 **Murder**
8 **Parliament**
9 **Plague**
10 **Pod**

☆ Answers on page 183

11 **Pride**

12 **Shrewdness**

13 **Smack**

14 **Streak**

15 **Unkindness**

Australia's States and Territories

Australia is composed of six states and two mainland territories, as marked on the map below. Can you label them?

☆ *Answers on page 183*

Coastlines

Below are the lengths (to the nearest 100m) of the ten longest coastlines around sovereign states. To which countries do the lengths correspond?

LENGTH (KM)	COUNTRY
202,100	
54,700	
37,700	
36,300	
29,800	
25,800	
25,100	
19,900	
15,100	
14,500	

Animal Young

Lots of animals breed to produce calves or pups and the like, but a few animals have more unusual names assigned to their young. Ten of these animals are listed below. What are their offspring called?

1 **Beaver**
2 **Deer**
3 **Dragonfly**
4 **Goat**
5 **Goose**
6 **Kangaroo**

☆ Answers on pages 183–4

7 Swan

8 Eel

9 Hare

10 Owl

Anniversaries

Traditionally, each year of marriage is symbolized by
a different material. Can you name the material associated
with each anniversary below?

First

Second

Third

Fifth

Tenth

Fifteenth

Twentieth

Twenty-Fifth

Thirtieth

Thirty-Fifth

Fortieth

Forty-Fifth

Fiftieth

Fifty-fifth

Sixtieth

Answers on page 184

☆ Grand Slams ☆

Golf and tennis each have their own 'Grand Slams', a rarely achieved feat where a competitor holds several specific championships at one time. But what are the events that make up the Grand Slam in the case of each sport?

TENNIS   **GOLF**

The Books of Roald Dahl

Roald Dahl created some of the most popular books for children ever published. Can you name the titles in which the following characters appeared?

Aunt Sponge and Aunt Spiker
Victor Hazell
The Reverend Lee
Grandma Kranky
Gus, a fighter pilot
Little Billy
Sophie
Solveg and Ranghild
Charlie Bucket
Vermicious Knids
Mrs Phelps
Boggis, Bunce and Bean

☆ Answers on page 184

World's Longest Mountain Ranges

There are nine overground mountain ranges with peaks over 6,000 metres. In descending height order, can you name the five longest ranges in the world?

LENGTH (KM)	RANGE
7,200	
4,800	
3,800	
3,600	
3,500	

The Twelve Disciples

Do you know the names of Jesus's twelve apostles, as detailed (with slight variations between them) in the Four Gospels – Matthew, Mark, Luke and John.

Answers on pages 184–5

Complete the Proverbs

We all like to share the occasional pearl of wisdom. Here are some of the best, but missing key words. How should they read?

A little ___ is a dangerous thing.

Beware of ____ bearing ____.

Don't count your ____ before they've ____.

Let sleeping ____ lie.

Never judge a ____ by its ____.

Revenge is a ____ best served ____.

You can't make a ___ ___ from a ____ ____.

A ____ and his ____ are soon parted.

____ is in the eye of the ____.

____ is the better part of ____.

It's the early ____ that gets the ____.

Mighty ____ from little ____ grow.

People who live in ____ ____ shouldn't throw ____.

Too many ____ spoil the ____.

____ makes the ____ grow fonder.

____ is next to godliness.

Don't upset the ____ ____.

Make ____ while the sun ____.

One man's ____ is another man's ____.

Tell the ____ and shame the ____.

☆ Answers on page 185

If You Want to Get Ahead ...

Below are pictures of fifteen different types of hat popular through the ages. Can you correctly label each one?

A

B

C

D

E

F

G

H

I

J

K

L

M

N

☆ Answers on page 186

The Winter Olympics

The Winter Olympic Games were first held in 1924.
Can you match the years to the host city?

YEAR	HOST CITY
1924	
1928	
1932	
1936	
1948	
1952	
1956	
1960	
1964	
1968	
1972	
1976	
1980	
1984	
1988	
1992	
1994	
1998	
2002	
2006	
2010	
2014	

☆ Answers on page 186

Canadian Provinces and Territories

Canada is made up of thirteen distinct provinces and territories.
Can you label them correctly on the map below?

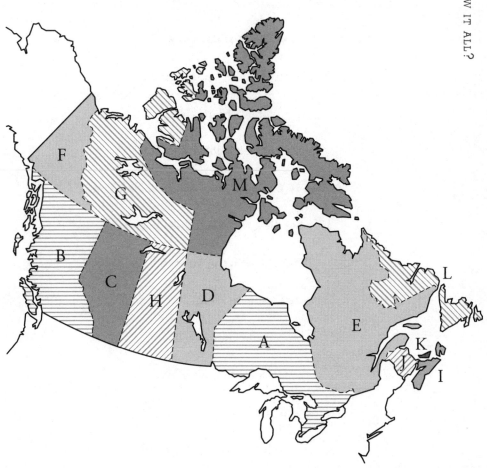

✑ *Answers on page 186*

Great Architects and Their Buildings

Below are the names and locations of fifteen iconic buildings.
All you have to do is name their famous architects.

Villa Rotonda, Vicenza

The White House, Washington, D.C.

Sydney Opera House

St Paul's Cathedral, London

Solomon R. Guggenheim Museum, New York

Sagrada Familia, Barcelona

Piazza San Pietro, Vatican City

Notre Dame du Haut, Ronchamp

India Gate, Delhi

Glasgow School of Art

Dome of Santa Maria del Fiore, Florence

Chrysler Building, New York

Bauhaus School, Dessau

Banqueting House, London

30 St Mary Axe ('The Gherkin'), London

☆ *Answers on page 187*

Baseball – the World Series

A total of twenty-two teams have triumphed in the World Series since its inauguration in 1903. Only eight teams have had five or more victories. Can you identify them from their total number of wins, and the first and most recent years that they were successful?

TOTAL WINS	FIRST WIN	LAST WIN	TEAM
27	1923	2009	
10	1926	2006	
9	1972	1989	
7	1912	2007	
6	1955	1988	
5	1905	1954	
5	1919	1990	
5	1909	1979	

The Characters of Enid Blyton

One of the most prolific children's authors in history, Enid Blyton created many memorable characters. Among the most popular were the Famous Five and the Secret Seven. But who were the members of the respective gangs?

FAMOUS FIVE   **SECRET SEVEN**

☆ *Answers on page 187*

The Canterbury Tales

Geoffrey Chaucer wrote *The Canterbury Tales* in the second half of the 14th century. By the time of his death he had completed twenty-four of the stories. But whose tales were they?

1
2
3
4
5
6
7
8
9
10
11
12
13
14
15
16
17
18
19
20
21
22
23
24

☆ *Answers on pages 187–8*

Rugby World Cup

To date, six teams have won the Rugby Union World Cup since
its inauguration in 1987. Can you remember which they are?

1987

1991

1995

1999

2003

2007

Demonyms

A demonym is the name given to the resident of any given locality. So,
for instance, a resident of New York has the demonym New Yorker.
But not all demonyms are so immediately obvious. Below are the
names of fifteen major cities. But what would you call an inhabitant?

Bologna

Cambridge

Cape Town

Caracas

Florence

Glasgow

Guadalajara

Ho Chi Minh City

Las Vegas

Liverpool

Mexico City

Moscow

Munich

Naples

Sydney

☆ *Answers on page 188*

The Complete Works of Gilbert and Sullivan

Gilbert and Sullivan, the most successful exponents
of light opera that ever lived, collaborated on a total
of fourteen operettas. Can you name them all?

1
2
3
4
5
6
7
8
9
10
11
12
13
14

☆ *Answers on page 188*

Types of Cloud

There are ten major cloud types – three 'high clouds' (with a base between 5,500 and 14,000 metres), three 'medium clouds' (between 2,000 and 7,000 metres) and four 'low clouds' (under 2,000 metres). Can you name them from the descriptions below?

HIGH CLOUDS

1 **White filaments**
2 **Small rippled elements**
3 **Transparent sheet (commonly with a halo)**

MEDIUM CLOUDS

4 **Layered, rippled elements, usually white with a degree of shading**
5 **Thin grey layer, showing the sun as if through crushed glass**
6 **A thick, dark layer, low base, from which it may rain or snow**

LOW CLOUDS

7 **A layered series of rounded rolls, mostly white with a little shading**
8 **Grey layers with a uniform base**
9 **Individual cells, vertical rolls or towers, with flat bases**
10 **Big towers, like cauliflowers with 'anvil tops', often bringing bad weather**

Answers on page 189

Wimbledon Tennis Champions

As of 2009, nine tennis players have won the Wimbledon Men's Singles
title more than once in the Open era. In descending order
of number of victories, can you name them all?

7

6

5

3

3

2

2

2

2

As of 2009, six competitors have won the Wimbledon Ladies' Singles
title more than once in the Open era. In descending order of number
of victories, can you name them all?

9

7

5

4

3

3

☆ Answers on page 189

Indian States

India is made up of twenty-eight states and seven union
territories. Can you name them?

STATES

◇◇◇

UNION TERRITORIES

◇◇◇

✫ Answers on pages 189–90

Computing Acronyms

The rise of information technology has generated a whole language of its own, liberally laced with confusing acronyms. Here are some of those that we have bandied about in recent years, but do you know what they stand for?

ADSL

BIOS

BMP

CD-ROM

CPU

DOS

DPI

DTD

GIGO

GPS

HTML

HTTP

IM

ISP

JPEG

Mbps

PDF

URL

USB

WWW

☆ *Answers on page 190*

The Novels of Charles Dickens

Charles Dickens was responsible for creating a cast of characters unrivalled in world literature. Can you name the book containing each of these characters?

Betsey Trotwood

Mr Bumble

Bob Cratchit

Mr Pecksniff

Madame Defarge

Abel Magwitch

Sam Weller

Wackford Squeers

Daniel Quilp

Gabriel Varden

Susan Nipper

Esther Summerson

Thomas Gradgrind

John Chivery

Lizzie Hexam

Rev. Septimus Crisparkle

✩ Answers on page 190

The Six Wives of Henry VIII

Henry VIII famously had six wives, whose fates are recalled in the rhyme: 'Divorced, beheaded, died; divorced, beheaded, survived.' In the order in which they married him, what were their names?

Roman Numerals

We see them all the time on clocks or at the end of the credits on TV, but the Roman numeral system remains a mystery to many. Can you remember which letters represent which numbers? There is also a sum at the end to test how well you really know the system ...

I

5

10

50

100

500

1000

MCDLIX – XXIV = ?

☆ Answers on page 191

Gods of Greek and Roman Mythology

Despite different names, the gods of Greek and Roman mythology could often be substituted one for another. From the descriptions below, can you name the god in both traditions?

DESCRIPTION	GREEK	ROMAN
King of the Gods		
God of the Sea		
God of the Underworld		
Goddess of the Hearth and Home		
God of War		
Goddess of War and Wisdom		
Sun God and God of Music and Archery		
Goddess of Love and Beauty		
Messenger of the Gods		
Goddess of the Moon, Childbirth and Hunting		
God of Fire		
God of Wine		
God of Love		
God of Sleep		

✄ *Answers on page 191*

The Crew of the USS Enterprise in the Original Star Trek

The USS *Enterprise*, the vessel beloved of all *Star Trek* fans, first boldly came on to our screens in 1966. Listed below are the posts held by that original crew. Can you name the character that filled each post and (to test your Trekkie credentials) the actor that played the role?

POSITION	ROLE	ACTOR
Captain		
First Officer/Science Officer		
Chief medical officer		
Chief engineer		
Communications officer		
Helmsman		
Navigator		
Captain's Yeoman		
Head Nurse		

Capital Cities of Asia

Here are twenty of Asia's countries.
But what are their capital cities?

1 **Afghanistan**

2 **Azerbaijan**

3 **Bangladesh**

4 **Bhutan**

5 **Cambodia**

6 **China**

7 **India**

8 **Indonesia**

9 **Japan**

10 **Korea (North)**

11 **Korea (South)**

12 **Malaysia**

13 **Mongolia**

14 **Nepal**

15 **Pakistan**

16 **Philippines**

17 **Thailand**

18 **Turkmenistan**

19 **Uzbekistan**

20 **Vietnam**

☆ *Answers on page 192*

Musical Notation

Below are a number of symbols commonly used in music manuscripts.
Can you name each symbol?

The Fellowship of the Lord of the Rings

In J.R.R. Tolkien's perennially popular *Lord of the Rings* series of books,
the Fellowship of the Ring consisted of nine members. We have given
you the race of each member. Can you provide the name?

RACE	NAME
Dwarf	
Elf	
Hobbit	
Hobbit	
Hobbit	
Hobbit	
Man	
Man	
Wizard	

Brothers and Sisters

Cane and Abel aside, some siblings have managed to work together to achieve great success. Can you recall the names of the siblings that made up the following well-known family units?

MARX BROTHERS

GIBB BROTHERS (THE BEEGEES)

ANDREWS SISTERS

BEVERLEY SISTERS

OSMONDS

JONAS BROTHERS

☆ *Answers on pages 192–3*

The Earth's Atmosphere

Earth's atmosphere is divided into five basic layers on the basis of their height above the planet's surface. Do you know what each layer is called?

HEIGHT ABOVE EARTH'S SURFACE	LAYER
5 miles at poles; 7 miles at mid-latitude; 10 miles at equator	
30 miles	
50 miles	
400 miles	
Up to 40,000 miles	

Dinosaurs

The name 'dinosaur' means, literally, 'monstrous lizard'. Can you identify the specific types of dinosaur being described here by the translations of their names?

Double-Beamed Lizard
Egg Thief
Face with Three Horns
Fish Lizard
Iguana Tooth
Roof Lizard
Speedy Robber
Strange Lizard
Tyrant Lizard King
Winged Lizard

☆ Answers on page 193

☆ **Royal Houses** ☆

Monarchies continue to thrive in many countries around the
world. Below are the names of several major ruling families.
In which countries do they reign?

ROYAL HOUSE	COUNTRY
Al Khalifa	
Wettin (Saxe-Coburg-Gotha line)	
Wangchuck	
Schleswig-Holstein-Sonderburg-Glücksburg	
Windsor	
Grimaldi	
Alaouite	
Orange-Nassau	
Saud	
Bourbon	
Dlamini	
Bernadotte	
Chakri	
Tupou	

Type-Cast

The layout of a standard English keyboard is based on the
typewriter layout devised by Milwaukee newspaper editor,
Christopher Sholes. Starting with the letter Q in the top left
corner, can you reproduce the exact order of letters?

☆ *Answers on pages 193–4*

International Time Zones

GMT (or Greenwich Meantime) is measured from the Greenwich Meridian Line at the Royal Observatory in London (on line of longitude 0° 0' 0"). It is the traditional standard from which all other time zones are measured. Unadjusted for summer time, can you say how many hours + or - GMT the time is in the following cities?

Anchorage
Auckland
Beijing
Honolulu
Moscow
New Delhi
New York
Paris
Pretoria
Quito
Sydney
Tokyo

Chinese Animal Zodiac

Under this system, each year is designated an animal under a twelve-year rotating cycle. But what are the twelve animals?

☆ Answers on page 194

ISO Codes

The International Organization of Standardization attributes a two-letter code to every country in the world. These might be used, for example, in defining a country's Internet domain names. Can you work out which countries the following codes refer to?

AT

AU

BA

BF

CN

CZ

DE

EE

ES

HR

IE

MX

NL

PL

QA

SE

TD

VA

ZA

ZM

☆ *Answers on page 194*

I am, you are, he is ...

The most basic verb to learn in any language is the present tense of 'to be'. But can you remember how to decline the same verb in French, German, Italian and Spanish (which has two equivalent verbs to confuse things further)? Even if you can't, there'll be no detention!

ENGLISH
To be…
I am
You are
He/she/one is
We are
You are
They are

FRENCH

GERMAN

ITALIAN

SPANISH

☆ Answers on page 195

The Novels of the Brontë Sisters

The three Brontë women – Anne, Charlotte and Emily – wrote a total of eight novels between them. Can you a) give the pen name of each sister and b) the names of each of their novels?

ANNE

Pen Name:
Novels
(1847)
(1848)

CHARLOTTE

Pen Name:
Novels
(1833)
(1834)
(1847)
(1849)
(1853)
(1857)

EMILY

Pen Name:
Novel
(1847)

Answers on page 195

Who Was on Drums?

Only a few bands have become so famous that the world at large
has had an idea of the names of all the members, as opposed to just
the singer or lead guitarist. Here are some of the greatest bands
of all time. Can you name the classic line-ups of each?
(The number in brackets gives you the number of band members.)

The Beatles (4)

Fleetwood Mac (4)

Abba (4)

The Jackson 5 (6 – one brother was replaced by another)

U2 (4)

The Monkees (4)

Queen (4)

☆ Answers on pages 195–6

The Moon's Seas

Our moon is home to several *maria*, or seas, which are in fact dark lava plains. Nine of these have diameters in excess of 500km. Do you know their English (as opposed to Latin) names?

DIAMETER	NAME
2570 km	
1600 km	
1120 km	
910 km	
870 km	
720 km	
710 km	
600 km	
510 km	

The G7

The G7 (Group of Seven) is an international organization comprising the world's seven largest economies. Can you name all the member states?

🌟 *Answers on page 196*

The Monopoly Board

One of the most popular board games of all time, Monopoly hit the market in the 1930s. The classic US version was based on locations in and around Atlantic City, while the British version looked towards London. But which locations correspond to which colours?

US EDITION		UK EDITION	
COLOUR	LOCATION NAME	COLOUR	LOCATION NAME
Purple		Brown	
Purple		Brown	
Light blue		Light blue	
Light blue		Light blue	
Light blue		Light blue	
Pink		Purple	
Pink		Purple	
Pink		Purple	
Orange		Orange	
Orange		Orange	
Orange		Orange	
Red		Red	
Red		Red	
Red		Red	
Yellow		Yellow	
Yellow		Yellow	
Yellow		Yellow	
Green		Green	
Green		Green	
Green		Green	
Dark blue		Dark blue	
Dark blue		Dark blue	

☆ Answers on page 197

Semaphore Signals

Developed in the late eighteenth century by Claude Chappe,
Semaphore uses a system of hand-held flags or lights to
communicate a message. Can you read the message below?

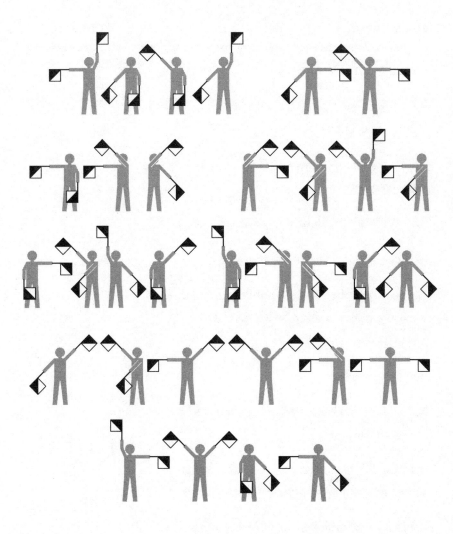

Landlocked Nations

There are forty-two landlocked nations on Earth, i.e. countries with no coastline. Below are listed the neighbours of ten of these countries. Can you work out which countries are being described?

BORDERED BY	COUNTRY
Bolivia, Brazil and Argentina	
Burundi, Democratic Republic of the Congo, Uganda and Tanzania	
China, Vietnam, Cambodia, Thailand and Myanmar	
Eritrea, Djibouti, Somalia, Kenya and Sudan	
Georgia, Azerbaijan, Turkey and Iran	
Germany and the Czech Republic, Slovakia, Hungary, Slovenia, Italy, Switzerland and Liechtenstein	
Italy	
Russia, China, Uzbekistan, Kyrgyzstan and Turkmenistan	
Slovakia, Ukraine, Romania, Croatia, Serbia and Montenegro, Slovenia and Austria	
Zambia, Mozambique, South Africa, Botswana and Namibia	

☆ *Answers on page 197*

World's Largest Countries

Can you name the ten largest countries in the world by area?

AREA (SQ KM)	COUNTRY
17,075,000	
9,976,000	
9,629,000	
9,597,000	
8,512,000	
7,687,000	
3,288,000	
2,767,000	
2,718,000	
2,506,000	

Days of the Week in Different Languages

A test of how much attention you were paying in language lessons. Very simply, can you come up with the days of the week in French, German, Spanish and Italian?

ENGLISH	FRENCH	GERMAN	SPANISH	ITALIAN
Monday				
Tuesday				
Wednesday				
Thursday				
Friday				
Saturday				
Sunday				

Answers on page 198

United Nations
Secretary Generals

Since its establishment in 1945, the United Nations has had
eight Secretary Generals. Here are their terms of office, but can
you name each one, along with their country of origin?

TERM OF OFFICE	NAME	NATIONALITY
1946–1952		
1953–1961		
1961–1971		
1972–1981		
1982–1991		
1992–1997		
1997–2007		
2007–		

Chess Pieces

In a game of chess each player has sixteen pieces. Given the
quantity of each piece per player, can you recall the names?

NO. OF PIECES	NAME
1	
1	
2	
2	
2	
8	

☆ Answers on page 198

Who Said What? (Part I)

Here are some well-known quotes by some of the most famous people who ever lived. So who said what?

'I have a dream that my four little children will one day live in a nation where they will not be judged by the color of their skin, but by the content of their character.'

'Better to remain silent and be thought a fool than to speak out and remove all doubt.'

'Strive not to be a success, but rather to be of value.'

'A lie can run around the world six times while the truth is still trying to put on its pants.'

'The true end of tragedy is to purify the passions.'

'Hatred can be overcome only by love.'

'Youth is wasted on the young.'

'In War: Resolution. In Defeat: Defiance. In Victory: Magnanimity. In Peace: Goodwill.'

'If you judge people, you have no time to love them.'

'We're more popular than Jesus now; I don't know which will go first – rock and roll or Christianity.'

✮ *Answers on pages 198–9*

Musical Terms

Here are the meanings of some terms commonly used to indicate pace in musical manuscripts. Do you know their names?

MEANING	TERM
Very slow	
Slow	
Moderately slow	
'Walking' tempo	
Fast	
Lively	
Very fast	
Moderate(ly)	
Gradually becoming faster	
Gradually becoming slower	

The Heptathlon

The classic outdoor women's heptathlon consists of seven events. What are they?

☆ *Answers on page 199*

International Airport Codes

Every major airport in the world has a designated three-letter International Air Transport Association code. Where would you be flying to if your destination airport had the following codes?

CODE	CITY (AIRPORT NAME)
ARN	
BNE	
BOM	
CDG	
DXB	
GDL	
GIG	
JFK	
LAX	
LHR	
LOS	
NRT	
SVO	
TXL	
YVR	

⭐ *Answers on page 199*

Putting a Name to a Dish

A few select people have had a foodstuff, drink or recipe named after them. From the descriptions below, can you work out who was the honoured party in each case?

An English biscuit named after a nineteenth-century Italian patriot

A type of tea with a distinctive bergamot tang named after a British prime minister of the 1830s

A classic pizza named in honour of the wife of Umberto I of Italy in 1889

A mix of fruit and ice cream created in recognition of an Australian operatic soprano

A meringue dessert inspired by a Russian ballerina

A popular bread-based snack named after John Montagu, an eighteenth-century English aristocrat

A tuber developed in the early years of the twentieth century and named after the British monarch whose coronation was in 1902

A dish of beef, pâté and mushrooms in pastry, named after a British military hero

A versatile vegetable dish popularized in Britain during a period of wartime rationing and named after the then Minister of Food

☆ *Answers on pages 199–200*

Disney Feature Films

Before his death in 1967, Walt Disney oversaw the production of nineteen films included in the Disney Animated Classics canon. Given the dates of release, can you name them all?

YEAR	FILM
1937	
1940	
1940	
1941	
1942	
1942	
1944	
1946	
1947	
1948	
1949	
1950	
1951	
1953	
1955	
1959	
1961	
1963	
1967	

☆ *Answers on page 200*

Who Lives There?

Below are twenty famous addresses, some real and some fictional.
Can you name the resident(s) of each one?

ADDRESS	RESIDENT(S)
10 Downing Street	
North Cemetery Ridge, USA	
110a Piccadilly, London	
Danemead, High Street, St Mary Mead	
112 ½ Beacon Street, Boston	
Neverland, Santa Barbara County, CA	
1600 Pennsylvania Avenue	
1938 Sullivan Place, Metropolis, USA	
221B Baker Street	
Puddleby-on-the-Marsh, Slopshire, England	
23 Railway Cuttings, East Cheam	
32 Windsor Gardens, London	
Southfork Ranch, Braddock County, Texas	
4 Privet Drive, Little Whinging, Surrey	
518 Crestview Drive, Beverly Hills, California	
565 North Clinton Drive, Milwaukee, WI	
Wayne Manor, Gotham City	
62 West Wallaby Street, Wigan, Lancs	
698 Candlewood Lane, Cabot Cove, ME	
742 Evergreen Terrace, Springfield	

☆ Answers on pages 200–201

Ologies

If you want to impress someone, a guaranteed way is to be a specialist in an '-ology'. But what do they all mean? Here are a few to test your pantology.

'-OLOGY'	AREA OF STUDY
Anthropology	
Arachnology	
Campanology	
Cardiology	
Conchology	
Dermatology	
Geology	
Gerontology	
Haematology	
Meteorology	
Nephology	
Oncology	
Oology	
Ophthalmology	
Ornithology	
Osteology	
Palaeontology	
Pharmacology	
Seismology	
Vexillology	

Answers on page 201

☆ Hits of The Beatles ☆

The Beatles had an amazing twenty-seven number-one
singles in the UK and USA. Can you recall them all?

1+1=2

Here are the names of one half of some of the most famous
double acts. For each one, can you identify the missing partner?

Beavis
Bing Crosby
Bud Abbott
'Cheech' Marin
Dean Martin
Dudley Moore
Ernie Wise
Ginger Rogers
Gracie Allen
Ike
Lennie Peters
Penn Jillette

☆ *Answers on pages 201–2*

Renée
Sonny Bono
Stephen Fry

African Capitals

Here is a list of the capital cities of twenty African nations.
But what are their countries?

CAPITAL	COUNTRY
Abuja	
Addis Ababa	
Asmara	
Bamako	
Cairo	
Dakar	
Freetown	
Harare	
Kampala	
Khartoum	
Kigali	
Luanda	
Lusaka	
Mogadishu	
Monrovia	
Nairobi	
Ouagadougou	
Rabat	
Tripoli	
Windhoek	

✭ Answers on page 202

Geographical Terms

Were you paying attention when the teacher explained
what all those funny geographical terms actually meant?
Below are several definitions – can you remember the
terms to which they refer?

1 A pair of points on opposite sides of the planet

2 A narrow strip of land connecting two bigger landmasses

3 A stretch of lowland between mountains, hills or other
uplands

4 A narrow body of water connecting two larger water
bodies

5 A chain or cluster of islands in an ocean

6 A pointed piece of land that sticks out into a body
of water

7 The imaginary line that circles the world at the mid-
point between the North and South Poles

8 A ring of coral forming an island in the sea

9 An area of land surrounded by water on three sides

10 A river or stream flowing into a larger river

☆ *Answers on page 202*

Famous Ships and Boats

Here are clues to the identity of fifteen famous (real-life and fictional) sailing vessels. Can you work out which they are?

Warship in the navy of King Henry VIII of England that sank off the south coast

Passenger liner that sank on its maiden voyage to New York in 1912, with huge loss of life

The ship featured in Robert Louis Stevenson's *Treasure Island*

Captain Ahab's whaling ship in *Moby Dick*

Cunard liner that sank in 1915, contributing to the USA's entry into the First World War

Greenpeace ship sunk by French operatives in 1985

Cunard's flagship liner from 1969 until 2004

Lord Nelson's flagship at the Battle of Trafalgar

Famous nineteenth-century tea clipper now in dry dock at Greenwich in London

Flagship of the English pirate Blackbeard

Cruiser that played a crucial role in the October Revolution in Russia in 1917

Ship that carried the Pilgrims from England to Plymouth, Massachusetts, in 1620

☆ *Answers on pages 202–3*

The ship on which Charles Darwin carried out much of his most famous work and whose name appeared in the title of one of his books

Raft used by Thor Heyerdahl for his epic 1947 voyage.

Name of Jason's ship in classical mythology

Muppets

The Muppets were the creation of the genius puppeteer, Jim Henson. Countless children have grown up watching them but can you remember who was who in the show from these descriptions?

Host and director of the show

A glamour-pig with a thing for the host

A bear that does stand-up comedy

The company's factotum and nephew to the theatre owner

A daredevil with a prominent nose

A piano-playing dog

A strange drumming creature

The science officer in *Pigs in Space*

Assistant to the inventor, Dr. Bunsen Honeydew

The old men who heckle from one of the theatre boxes

☆ *Answers on page 203*

Boys and Girls

Can you work out what names are given to the male and
female of the following species?

SPECIES	MALE	FEMALE
Deer		
Donkey		
Goat		
Hedgehog		
Swan		
Duck		
Peafowl		
Sheep		
Zebra		

Ivy League

The Ivy League is a network of eight elite colleges in the
northeast of the USA. What are their names?

☆ Answers on page 203

Temperature Scales

Three of the most common scales of temperature that we use are Celcius, Farenheit and Kelvin. But how hot is hot? Here is a short list of key temperature indicators. Can you say what they are in Farenheit and Kelvin?

DESCRIPTION	°C	°F	K
Water boils	100		
Body temperature	37		
Room temperature	21		
Freezing point of water	0		

The Works of Oscar Wilde

Below are listed characters from major works by Oscar Wilde. Can you remember the works in which they appeared?

Lord Darlington

Mrs Arbuthnot

Herod

Mrs Cheveley

Miss Prism

Basil Hallward

Hiram B. Otis

☆ Answers on pages 203–4

The Organs of the Body

To test your knowledge of human anatomy, can you correctly label the internal organs marked on this diagram of a human being?

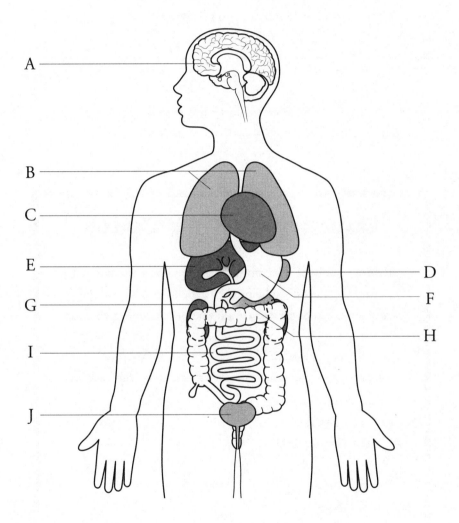

☆ *Answers on page 204*

☆ The Hits of ☆ Michael Jackson

Michael Jackson achieved sixteen US or UK number-one singles, the first in 1972 and the last in 1997. How many of them can you remember?

Country Calling Codes

The International Telecommunication Union ascribes each country with a code to be used by callers from abroad. How many do you know? Here are a few countries to test you out.

COUNTRY	CODE
Australia	
Brazil	
France	
Germany	
India	
Nigeria	
Russia	
South Africa	
UK	
USA	

☆ Answers on page 204

The Great Lakes

There are five North American Great Lakes.
Can you name them all, from largest to smallest?

Santa's Reindeer

According to the poem, 'A Visit from St. Nicholas',
what were the names of Santa's eight reindeer?

Cluedo

One of the most enduring board games ever invented,
Cluedo provides an opportunity to unleash the Sherlock Holmes
in all of us. Can you remember the names of the six suspects,
the possible scenes of crimes and the potential murder weapons?

SUSPECTS

ROOMS

WEAPONS

✰ *Answers on page 205*

Infamous Assassinations

Below is a list of assassins who have blotted the course of history. Can you name their principal victim in each case?

ASSASSIN	VICTIM
Yigal Amir	
John Wilkes Booth	
Brutus	
Mark Chapman	
Nathuram Godse	
Talmadge Hayer	
Lee Harvey Oswald	
Gavrilo Princip	
James Earl Ray	
Sirhan Sirhan	

Famous Explorers

In an era of easy travel that means we can get from one end of the world to the other in a day, it is easy to forget that we relied on many brave individuals to map the world for us. Can you identify the famous explorers from the mini-biographies below?

Italian-born explorer who sailed extensively around South America from c. 1497 to 1505 and after whom America is said to have been named.

An Italian who famously travelled to China (then known as Cathay) via the Silk Road and resided for years at the court of Kublai Khan.

Spanish explorer best known for seizing the Aztec Empire for his country in the first half of the sixteenth century.

Dutch explorer who discovered New Zealand and who gave his name to one of Australia's states.

The man who set out to find a new route to India and stumbled upon America instead.

A captain who claimed the east coast of Australia for Britain, charted Newfoundland and New Zealand and was the first European to discover Hawaii (named the Sandwich Islands). Also helped find a way of preventing scurvy.

A Chinese explorer who made seven voyages to the Indian Ocean between 1405 and 1433, covering 35,000 miles and travelling to over thirty different Asian and African countries.

A one-time favourite of Elizabeth I, whose explorations of the Americas were interspersed with imprisonment in the Tower of London. He was ultimately beheaded.

Sailing under the Spanish flag, he is credited as the first person to circumnavigate the world (though he died before docking back in Spain in 1521).

A Victorian-era Scottish missionary who explored central Africa and became the first European to set eyes on Victoria Falls.

Back in the USSR

The Soviet Union was, for most of its existence,
made up of fifteen constituent states. Can you name
all fifteen (using their post-Soviet names), along with
their capital cities?

STATE	CAPITAL CITY

London Tube Lines

The London Underground is the oldest underground railway system in the world. Do you know the names of all eleven lines and can you match them correctly to their colours?

LINE COLOUR	NAME
Light blue	
Red	
Yellow	
Pink	
Brown	
Green	
Dark magenta	
Silver	
Black	
Dark blue	
Turquoise	

The Hits of Madonna

One of the great cultural icons of the late-twentieth and early twenty-first centuries, Madonna had achieved twelve number-one hit singles in her native USA by January 2010. What are they?

✮ *Answers on page 206*

The Ten Commandments

At the heart of the Bible are the Ten Commandments that
Moses received on Mount Sinai. Can you remember them
(as set down in Exodus 20)?

So What Exactly Do You Do?

Here is a list of several job titles, some of which are now rather
antiquated. What do/did these professionals actually do?

1 **Chandler**
2 **Hostler**
3 **Cooper**
4 **Keeler**
5 **Scrivener**
6 **Tanner**
7 **Wainwright**
8 **Draper**
9 **Costermonger**
10 **Chiffonier**
11 **Thatcher**

☆ Answers on page 207

Quotes From the Movies

We all have those moments when we wish we could deliver a great line like they do in the movies. But which films do the following quotes come from?

'A census taker once tried to test me. I ate his liver with some fava beans and a nice chianti.'

'Of all the gin joints in all the towns in all the world, she walks into mine.'

'You don't understand! I coulda had class. I coulda been a contender. I could've been somebody, instead of a bum, which is what I am.'

'Love means never having to say you're sorry.'

'Frankly, my dear, I don't give a damn.'

'There's no place like home.'

'I'm king of the world!'

'Why don't you come up sometime and see me?'

'Lunch is for Wimps.'

'Carpe diem. Seize the day, boys. Make your lives extraordinary.'

Answers on page 207

National Flags

Here are twenty-five flags from around the world.
Can you name the countries?

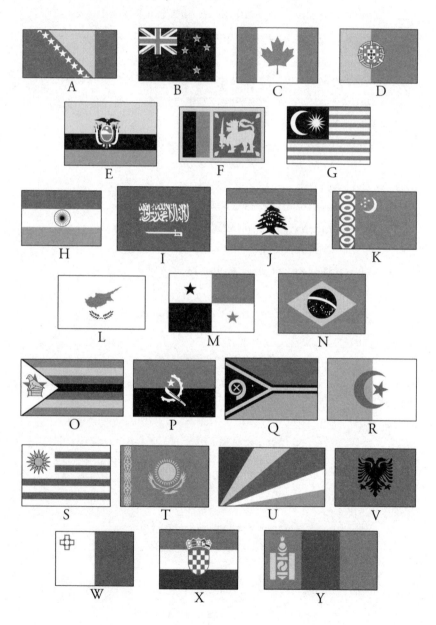

☆ Answers on page 208

Jazz Soubriquets

In the world of jazz, it seems as though it is essential to have a super cool nickname before you can really make it. Below are ten greats, who all had nicknames (which for some would become better known than their real names). Can you remember their made-up monikers?

1 Billie Holiday
2 Charlie Parker
3 Eddie Davis
4 Edward Kennedy Ellington
5 Ferdinand Morton
6 Jean Reinhardt
7 John Birks Gillespie
8 Julian Adderley
9 Thomas Waller
10 William Basie

The Planet's Biggest Deserts

According to the World Almanac, there are seven non-polar deserts with an area of over 150,000 square miles. Can you name them, from largest to smallest?

☆ Answers on page 208

The Boroughs of New York

The city that never sleeps is comprised of five distinct boroughs. What are they?

City Nicknames

There are many cities throughout the world that have their own nicknames. Can you work out which cities are being referred to here?

NICKNAME	CITY
The Big Easy	
City of a Thousand Minarets	
City of Dreaming Spires	
City of the Seven Hills	
Motor City	
Queen of the Adriatic	
Sin City	
The Big Apple	
The Forbidden City	
Windy City	

☆ Answers on page 209

☆ The Movies of ☆
Steven Spielberg

Steven Spielberg is one of the most successful directors
in Hollywood history, though his work has not always
been recognized at the Oscars. Seven of his films have been
nominated for best picture. What were they (and which was
the only one that won)?

The Continents

The World is divided up into seven distinct continents.
Can you name them all?

☆ Answers on page 209

South American Capitals

Below is a list of South American nations.
Can you name their capital cities?

NATION	CAPTIAL CITY
Argentina	
Brazil	
Chile	
Colombia	
Ecuador	
Guyana	
Paraguay	
Peru	
Uruguay	
Venezuela	

Sacred Texts

At the heart of virtually every major religion is scripture –
sacred texts to guide the believers. Can you name the faiths
with which the following texts are associated?

1 **Adi Granth**

2 **Kalpasutra**

3 **Kojiki**

4 **Mahabharata**

5 **New Testament**

6 **Pali Tipitaka**

7 **Qur'an**

8 **Talmud**

9 **Tao Te Ching**

☆ *Answers on pages 209–10*

Stevenson's
Treasure Island

Robert Louis Stevenson's classic children's adventure,
Treasure Island, was published in 1883. Can you identify
its main protagonists from the descriptions below?

*The novel's chief narrator and son of the landlords of the
The Admiral Benbow Inn*

Good-hearted but loose-tongued financier of the treasure hunt

The upstanding and ultimately brave captain of the Hispaniola

Employed as the Hispaniola's *cook, he leads the mutiny*

A bedraggled, former pirate marooned on the island for three years

An evil one-eyed pirate who meets his end under the hooves of a horse

Described by Stevenson as 'the bloodthirstiest buccaneer that sailed'

*An upright and cool-headed medic, in large part responsible for the
expedition's success*

Famously received the Black Spot and died of fear

✩ *Answers on page 210*

Famous Couples

History is littered with great romantic couples.
Below are a few 'halves'. Can you name the partner
who makes up the 'whole'?

Pharaoh Akhenaten
Humphrey Bogart
Napoleon Bonaparte
Robert Browning
Kurt Cobain
Shah Jahan
John Lennon
Prince Ranier
Samson
Edward VIII

Novels of Jane Austen

Jane Austen, that great chronicler of early nineteenth-century
mores, published six novels. What were they?

YEAR PUBLISHED	NOVEL
1811	
1813	
1814	
1815	
1818	
1818	

☆ *Answers on page 210*

Great Works of Philosophy

Philosophers, the great thinkers of our species, have
thankfully translated their ideas on to paper for millennia.
Can you name the authors of the following works?

An Enquiry Concerning Human Understanding

Beyond Good and Evil

Candide

The Origin of Species

Leviathan

Mathematical Principles of Natural Philosophy

Meditations on First Philosophy

Philosophical Investigations

Summa Theologica

The Communist Manifesto

The Critique of Pure Reason

The Nicomachean Ethics

The Prince

The Republic

Utopia

☆ *Answers on page 210*

Scientific Breakthroughs

Below are descriptions of ten of the greatest scientific
thinkers in history. Can you name them?

*British computer scientist often identified as the inventor
of the World Wide Web.*

The genius behind the theory of relativity.

*The first man to accurately describe the circulation
of blood around the body.*

*Danish recipient of the Nobel Prize for Physics for his
work on atomic structure.*

*French chemist and microbiologist who made significant
breakthroughs in identifying disease causes and preventions
(including a vaccination against rabies).*

*Reputedly had an apple to thank for putting him on to his
theory of universal gravitation.*

A naturalist who developed the theory of natural selection.

Austrian godfather of the psychology of the unconscious.

*Author of the most widely read book ever published on the
science of the Big Bang and black holes.*

*Sixteenth-century astronomer who outlined his theory of the heliocentric
cosmos, in which the Earth is not at the centre of the Universe.*

☆ *Answers on page 211*

Parts of Speech

How much grammar did you learn from your school days?
Can you identify the basic parts of speech that make up language?

EXAMPLE	PART OF SPEECH
to be	
dog	
quickly	
we	
beautiful	
in	
and	
Cheers!	

☆ Comic Book Alter Egos ☆

Everybody loves a superhero but can you recognize the
daredevils below from their day-to-day identities?

CIVILIAN NAME	HERO NAME
Bruce Banner	
Billy Batson	
Johnny Blaze	
Dick Grayson	
James Howlett	
Clark Kent	
Peter Parker	
Diana Prince	
Steve Rogers	
Bruce Wayne	

 Answers on page 211

Orson Welles' Feature Films

Orson Welles is one of the greatest actors and directors of the twentieth
century, often credited with creating the greatest film of all time.
He made a dozen feature-length films. Can you name them all?

YEAR	FILM
1941	
1942	
1946	
1947	
1948	
1952	
1955	
1958	
1962	
1965	
1968	
1974	

Plate Tectonics

Earth's surface is made up of a rock crust floating on a fluid magma
bed, with the crust made up of several interlocking plates. There are
generally considered to be fifteen main plates. What are they called?

The Musicals of Andrew Lloyd Webber

Arguably the most successful exponent of the modern musical, Andrew Lloyd Webber splits critics but never lacks an audience. Between 1965 and 2010, he wrote the music for sixteen major shows. What are they?

1

2

3

4

5

6

7

8

9

10

11

12

13

14

15

16

☆ *Answers on page 212*

Who Recorded the Album?

Here are some of the bestselling and most influential albums ever recorded. But which artists were responsible for which records?

ALBUM (YEAR OF RELEASE)	ARTIST
Songs for Swingin' Lovers! (1956)	
A Love Supreme (1964)	
Pet Sounds (1966)	
I Never Loved a Man the Way I Love You (1967)	
Astral Weeks (1968)	
After the Goldrush (1970)	
Paranoid (1970)	
Arrival (1976)	
Songs in the Key of Life (1976)	
Trans-Europe Express (1977)	
Exodus (1977)	
Parallel Lines (1978)	
London Calling (1979)	
Synchronicity (1983)	
Graceland (1986)	
Sign o'the Times (1987)	
The Joshua Tree (1987)	
It Takes a Nation of Millions to Hold Us Back (1988)	
3 Feet High and Rising (1989)	
Blood Sugar Sex Magik (1991)	
Automatic for the People (1992)	
Parklife (1994)	
Jagged Little Pill (1995)	
Parachutes (2000)	
Elephant (2003)	

British Prime Ministers

Since Neville Chamberlain resigned as British Prime Minister in 1940, there have been fourteen changes of premier. Here are the dates of each period in office. You just need to insert the correct name and party affiliation.

TENURE	NAME	PARTY
1940–1945		
1945–1951		
1951–1955		
1955–1957		
1957–1963		
1963–1964		
1964–1970		
1970–1974		
1974–1976		
1976–1979		
1979–1990		
1990–1997		
1997–2007		
2007–		

✩ *Answers on page 213*

In a Galaxy Far, Far Away ...

George Lucas has made six episodes of the *Star Wars* saga
into action movies. Can you name them?

EPISODE (YEAR OF THEATRICAL RELEASE)	TITLE
I (1999)	
II (2002)	
III (2005)	
IV (1977)	
V (1980)	
VI (1983)	

Formula 1 Champions

To 2010, eight drivers had won three or more Formula 1 World Drivers'
Championships. Here are the years that they won.
You just need to fill in the names.

VICTORIES	DRIVER
1994, 1995, 2000, 2001, 2002, 2003, 2004	
1951, 1954, 1955, 1956, 1957	
1985, 1986, 1989, 1993	
1959, 1960, 1966	
1969, 1971, 1973	
1975, 1977, 1984	
1981, 1983, 1987	
1988, 1990, 1991	

☆ *Answers on page 213*

Lines From Shakespeare

He is the most famous writer in the English language and responsible for some of the most memorable lines ever committed to paper. But can you match the following quotes to the plays from which they came?

'If music be the food of love, play on.'

'To be, or not to be: that is the question.'

'Good night, good night! Parting is such sweet sorrow.'

'The better part of valor is discretion, in the which better part I have saved my life.'

'If you prick us do we not bleed? If you tickle us do we not laugh? If you poison us do we not die? And if you wrong us, shall we not revenge?'

'Out, damn'd spot! out, I say!'

'A horse, a horse! My kingdom for a horse!'

'Cry Havoc! and let slip the dogs of war.'

'If we shadows have offended,/Think but this, and all is mended,'

'Thereby hangs a tale.'

☆ *Answers on pages 213–14*

Who Said What? (Part II)

Here are some more famous quotes from the great and the good.
Can you identify the originators of these wise words?

*'I have walked that long road to freedom. I have tried not to falter;
I have made missteps along the way. But I have discovered the
secret that after climbing a great hill, one only finds that there
are many more hills to climb.'*

'Well behaved women rarely make history.'

*'Our greatest happiness does not depend on the condition of life in
which chance has placed us, but is always the result of a good conscience,
good health, occupation, and freedom in all just pursuits.'*

'Float like a butterfly, sting like a bee.'

'Nothing that is worth knowing can be taught.'

*'Others have seen what is and asked why. I have seen what could be
and asked why not.'*

*'A woman drove me to drink and I didn't even have the
decency to thank her.'*

*'Our greatest glory is not in never falling,
but in getting up every time we do.'*

'A room without books is like a body without a soul.'

*'I know I have the body of a weak and feeble woman,
but I have the heart and stomach of a king.'*

☆ *Answers on page 214*

Walking on the Moon

Since man first walked on the moon in 1969, there were hopes
that we might all be rocketing off there before long. As it has
turned out, only twelve men in total have felt the moon
under their feet, the last in 1972. Can you name the lucky few?

☆ Willy Wonka's ☆ Golden Ticket Winners

In Roald Dahl's *Charlie and the Chocolate Factory*,
five fortunate children received golden tickets to go and
visit Willy Wonka's factory. What were their names?

☆ *Answers on page 214*

World's Smallest Countries

Can you name the ten smallest sovereign countries
in the world by area?

AREA (SQ KM)	COUNTRY
316	
300	
261	
181	
160	
61	
26	
21	
2	
1	

Warsaw Pact Countries

The Warsaw Pact of 1955 militarily bound eight East
European countries together and cast a shadow over the
continent for over thirty-five years. But which were the
nations that signed up to it?

☆ *Answers on pages 214–5*

The Novels of Ernest Hemingway

One of the great (and indeed tough) men of American letters, Ernest Hemingway wrote ten novels in his life (three of which were published posthumously). Here are their years of publication. Can you fill in the titles?

YEAR	NOVEL
1926	
1926	
1929	
1937	
1940	
1950	
1952	
1970	
1986	
1999	

Friends

Friends was the US sitcom that *sooo* took over the world in the 1990s (not least by prompting a million attempts to copy the 'Rachel haircut'). But what were the names of the six lead characters, and who played them?

☆ *Answers on page 215*

Multiple 'Time' Person of the Year

The iconic *Time* magazine has named a 'Person of the Year' annually since 1927. A select few have even received the accolade more than once. Can you guess who they are from the years in which they won?

YEARS	NAME
1932, 1934, 1941	
1939, 1942	
1940, 1949	
1943, 1947	
1945, 1948	
1944, 1959	
1964, 1967	
1971, 1972	
1980, 1983	
1978, 1985	
1987, 1989	
1992, 1998	
2000, 2004	

Generic Product Names

Sometimes a brand achieves such success or market dominance
that its name becomes commonly accepted as the generic name for
a product. Can you work out the brand names described here?

PRODUCT	GENERIC NAME
Ballpoint pen	
Clear sticky tape	
Flying disc used as toy	
Hook-and-loop fastening	
Luxury recreational vehicle	
Plastic storage containers	
Raincoat	
Self-adhesive notelets	
Vacuum cleaner	
Whirlpool bath	

☆ Original US Colonies ☆

In 1783 Britain formally recognized the independence of the
thirteen colonies that formed the original United States
of America. But what were the thirteen?

☆ Answers on page 216

Egyptian Gods and Goddesses

The ancient Egyptians developed a complex religious system that prospered for several millennia before all but dying out with the rise of Christianity. Can you name the gods and goddesses listed below?

ROLE	NAME
King of the Gods	
Sun God	
Primal Creator	
God of the Afterlife	
Goddess of Fertility and Magic	
God of the Dead	
God of the Sky and the Pharaohs	
Goddess of the Sky	
Goddess of the Nile	
God of the Desert and Chaos	

☆ *Answers on page 216*

Stephen Sondheim Musicals

◆►◆◄◆

Stephen Sondheim is a living legend of the American musical. Between 1954 and 2010 he had written or co-written eighteen major works. How many can you recall?

✧ *Answers on pages 216–7*

Scales

Can you name the widely used scales employed to measure the following?

1 **Acidity/alkalinity of a solution**
2 **Force of hurricanes**
3 **Force of tornado**
4 **Health of newborn baby**
5 **Impaired consciousness**
6 **Mineral hardness**
7 **Sexuality**
8 **Sea swell and wave height**
9 **Seismic energy released in earthquake**
10 **Wind speed**

Tour de France Winners

The greatest cycling race in the world, eight men have won the Tour de France more than twice. Here are the years of their victories but what were their names?

YEARS	RIDER
1999, 2000, 2001, 2002, 2003, 2004, 2005	
1957, 1961, 1962, 1963, 1964	
1969, 1970, 1971, 1972, 1974	
1978, 1979, 1981, 1982, 1985	
1991, 1992, 1993, 1994, 1995	
1913, 1914, 1920	
1953, 1954, 1955	
1986, 1989, 1990	

☆ *Answers on page 217*

Heart Diagram

Here is a diagram of the human heart.
Can you name the areas labelled?

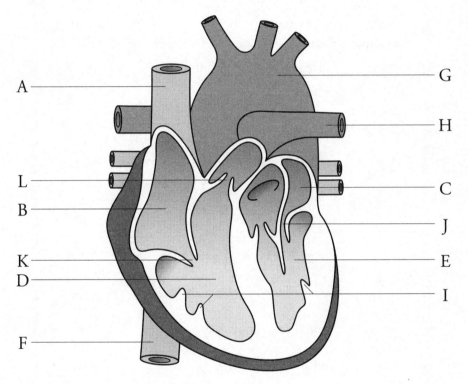

A

L

B

K

D

F

G

H

C

J

E

I

☆ *Answers on page 217*

Peace Treaties

Here are the details of various treaties that brought peace (if only temporarily) down through the ages. How many do you know?

DATE	OUTCOME	TREATY
843	Finalized partition of Carolingian Empire.	
1192	Ended Third Crusade.	
1559	Ended the Italian Wars.	
1648	Ended the Thirty Years' War and the Eighty Years' War.	
1713	Ended War of the Spanish Succession.	
1748	Ended War of the Austrian Succession.	
1842	Ended First Opium War.	
1848	Ended the Mexican-American War.	
1902	Ended Second Anglo-Boer War.	
1905	Ended the Russo-Japanese War.	
1996	Outlawed any nuclear explosion in any environment for military purposes.	

Book of the Movie

More often than not, if a film is made of a book it will keep the same title. But this is not always the case. Here are some notable films, but what were the names of the texts from which they were born?

FILM TITLE	LITERARY TITLE

A Cock and Bull Story
Adaptation
Apocalypse Now
Bladerunner
Cruel Intentions
Maybe Baby
Slumdog Millionaire
The Killing Fields
Village of the Damned
West Side Story

 **Space Shuttle Names**

NASA's Space Shuttle programme began in 1981 and by July 2009 had seen 129 flights by five different shuttles. What were the shuttles called?

☆ *Answers on page 218*

Art Galleries of the World

Below are some of the great art galleries of the world.
But in which cities would you find them?

1 Galleria Degli Uffizi
2 Groeninge Museum
3 Hermitage Museum
4 Hugh Lane Municipal Gallery
5 J. Paul Getty Museum
6 Metropolitan Museum of Art
7 Musée d'Orsay
8 Museo del Prado
9 Pushkin Museum of Fine Arts
10 Smithsonian American Art Museum
11 Tate Modern
12 The Altes Museum

Plagues of Egypt

The Book of Exodus describes ten plagues that befell Egypt.
What were they?

☆ Answers on page 218

Operas

W. H. Auden once noted, 'No good opera plot can be sensible, for people do not sing when they are feeling sensible.' Well, here are the titles of some of the best (along with their years of first performance). But who composed them?

OPERA	YEAR OF FIRST PERFORMANCE	COMPOSER
Don Giovanni	1787	
Fidelio	1805	
The Barber of Seville	1816	
Aida	1871	
Die Fledermaus	1874	
Eugene Onegin	1879	
Tosca	1900	
Ariadne auf Naxos	1912	
The Cunning Little Vixen	1924	
The Threepenny Opera	1928	
Peter Grimes	1945	
The Rake's Progress	1951	

⭐ *Answers on pages 218–19*

First Ladies

It is often said that behind every great man there is a great woman, and that has certainly proved to be the case with several US presidents. Can you name the post-Second World War First Ladies?

PRESIDENT	FIRST LADY
Harry S. Truman	
Dwight D. Eisenhower	
John F. Kennedy	
Lyndon B. Johnson	
Richard Nixon	
Gerald Ford	
Jimmy Carter	
Ronald Reagan	
George H. W. Bush	
Bill Clinton	
George W. Bush	
Barack Obama	

Nautical Terms

Are you sea-worthy? How many nautical terms can
you work out from the definitions below?

The front of a vessel.

The central structural member used in a ship's hull construction.

A unit of speed equivalent to one nautical mile per hour.

A unit of length, usually equivalent to three nautical miles.

The left-hand side of a vessel when facing forward.

The system of lines and masts on a sailing vessel.

The right-hand side of a vessel when facing forward.

*A line to show where the level of water should reach when
a ship is properly and fully loaded.*

A measurement (principally of depth) equivalent to six feet.

A ship's kitchen.

☆ *Answers on page 219*

Gold Medal Olympians

As of 2010, eleven athletes have won more than seven Olympic gold medals. Below are detailed their total number of golds, their events and nationalities. Can you identify the athlete?

MEDALS	EVENT	NATIONALITY	NAME
14	Swimming	USA	
9	Gymnastics	USSR	
9	Athletics	Finland	
9	Swimming	USA	
9	Athletics	USA	
8	Cross-country skiing	Norway	
8	Canoeing	E. Germany/Germany	
8	Gymnastics	Japan	
8	Swimming	USA	
8	Swimming	USA	
8	Athletics	USA	

☆ Answers on page 219

SI Units

SI units are internationally recognized units of measurement widely employed throughout science and commerce. There are seven base units representing various physical quantities. Do you know what they are?

PHYSICAL QUANTITY	UNIT
Length	
Mass	
Time	
Electric current	
Temperature	
Luminous intensity	
Amount of substance	

☆ Answers on page 219

FEELING CONFIDENT? LET'S SEE HOW WELL YOU'VE DONE ...

THE SOLAR SYSTEM

Mercury

Venus

Earth

Mars

Jupiter

Saturn

Uranus

Neptune

Pluto (which in 2006 was officially downgraded to a 'dwarf planet')

NAME THAT BIRD

A   Barn Owl

B   Blue Tit

C   Toucan

D   Coot

E   Cuckoo

F   Bald Eagle

G   Canada Goose

H   Jay

I   Kestrel

J   Kingfisher

K   Magpie

L   Mallard

M   Pheasant

N   Quail

O   Raven

P   Robin

Q   Swallow

R   Swift

S   Wood Pigeon

T   Wren

CUBE NUMBERS

1

8

27

64

125

216

343

512

729

1000

1331

1728

2197

2744

3375

FAMOUS FIRST LINES

Wuthering Heights,
    Emily Brontë

The Hound of the Baskervilles,
    Arthur Conan Doyle

Oliver Twist,
    Charles Dickens

Midnight's Children,
  Salman Rushdie

Atonement,
  Ian McEwan

Lucky Jim,
  Kingsley Amis

The Hitchhiker's Guide to
  the Galaxy, Douglas Adams

The Great Gatsby,
  F. Scott Fitzgerald

Little Women,
  Louisa May Alcott

The Stranger (L'Étranger),
  Albert Camus

November
Oscar
Papa
Quebec
Romeo
Sierra
Tango
Uniform
Victor
Whiskey
X-ray
Yankee
Zulu

THE PHONETIC ALPHABET

Alpha
Bravo
Charlie
Delta
Echo
Foxtrot
Golf
Hotel
India
Juliet
Kilo
Lima
Mike

THE HARRY POTTER NOVELS

Harry Potter and the
  Philosopher's Stone (1997)

Harry Potter and the
  Chamber of Secrets (1998)

Harry Potter and the
  Prisoner of Azkaban (1999)

Harry Potter and the
  Goblet of Fire (2000)

Harry Potter and the
  Order of the Phoenix (2003)

Harry Potter and the
  Half-Blood Prince (2005)

Harry Potter and the Deathly
  Hallows (2007)

TYING YOURSELF IN KNOTS

A Reef knot
B Sheet bend
C Figure of eight
D Round turn and two half-hitches
E Clove hitch
F Timber hitch
G Highwayman's hitch
H Sheepshank

THE SOCCER WORLD CUP

Team	Year(s)
Brazil	1958, 1962, 1970, 1994, 2002
Italy	1934, 1938, 1982, 2006
W. Germany	1954, 1974, 1990
Argentina	1978, 1986
Uruguay	1930, 1950
England	1966
France	1998

THE EUROPEAN UNION

Austria	Vienna
Belgium	Brussels
Bulgaria	Sofia
Cyprus	Nicosia
Czech Republic	Prague
Denmark	Copenhagen
Estonia	Tallinn
Finland	Helsinki
France	Paris
Germany	Berlin
Greece	Athens
Hungary	Budapest
Ireland	Dublin
Italy	Rome
Latvia	Riga
Lithuania	Vilnius
Luxembourg	Luxembourg
Malta	Valletta
Netherlands	Amsterdam
Poland	Warsaw
Portugal	Lisbon
Romania	Bucharest
Slovakia	Bratislava
Slovenia	Ljubljana
Spain	Madrid
Sweden	Stockholm
United Kingdom	London

BOOKS OF THE OLD TESTAMENT

Genesis

Exodus

Leviticus

Numbers

Deuteronomy

Joshua

Judges

Ruth

I Samuel

II Samuel

I Kings

II Kings

I Chronicles

II Chronicles

Ezra

Nehemiah

Esther

Job

Psalms

Proverbs

Ecclesiastes

Song of Solomon

Isaiah

Jeremiah

Lamentations

Ezekiel

Daniel

Hosea

Joel

Amos

Obadiah

Jonah

Micah

Nahum

Habakkuk

Zephaniah

Haggai

Zechariah

Malachi

WHAT'S IN A (CITY) NAME?

Beijing (China)

Chennai (India)

Dún Laoghaire (Ireland)

Faisalabad (Pakistan)

Gdańsk (Poland)

Harare (Zimbabwe)

Ho Chi Minh City (Vietnam)

Istanbul (Turkey)

Kinshasa (Dem. Rep. Congo)

New York (USA)

Oslo (Norway)

Seoul (South Korea)

St Petersburg (Russia)

Tokyo (Japan)

Yangon (Burma)

COLOURS OF
THE RAINBOW

Red

Orange

Yellow

Green

Blue

Indigo

Violet

FICTIONAL
CRIME-FIGHTING
SIDEKICKS

Sidekick / Creator

Robin / Bob Kane

R. Daneel Olivaw /
   Isaac Asimov

Tuppence Beresford /
   Agatha Christie

D. Sgt. Peter Pascoe /
   Reginald Hill

Dr John Watson /
   Arthur Conan Doyle

D. Sgt. Barbara Havers /
   Elizabeth George

Robbie Lewis / Colin Dexter

Cpt. Arthur Hastings /
   Agatha Christie

Det.Insp. Mike Burden /
   Ruth Rendell

Archie Goodwin / Rex Stout

Insp. Fox / Ngaio Marsh

INTERNATIONAL
AIRLINES

A Etihad Airways

B Qantas Airlines

C Thai Airways

D Virgin Atlantic

E Lufthansa

F Delta Airlines

G American Airlines

H Air Malta

I South African Airways

J British Midlands Airlines

K Aeroflot Airlines

L Air Canada

M Air France and KLM

N Tiger Airways

O Singapore Airlines

P Korean Air

Q Cathay Pacific

R Air China

S British Airways

T Emirates Airlines

GREAT COMPOSERS

Wolfgang Amadeus Mozart

Sergei Rachmaninoff

Pyotr Tchaikovsky

Ludwig Von Beethoven

Joseph Haydn

Johannes Brahms

Johann Sebastian Bach

Jan Sibelius

George Frédéric Handel

Frederic Chopin

Franz Schubert

Franz Liszt

Felix Mendelssohn

Antonio Vivaldi

Antonin Dvořák

ALL THE VOWELS

Abstemious

Abstentious

Acheilous

Anemious

Annelidous

Arsenious

Caesious

Facetious

THE EUROVISION SONG CONTEST

Artist / Year / Country

Dana / 1970 / Ireland

Lulu / 1969 / United Kingdom

Dana International / 1998 / Israel

Lordi / 2006 / Finland

Johnny Logan / 1987 / Ireland

Katrina and the Waves / 1997 / United Kingdom

Bucks Fizz / 1981 / United Kingdom

Céline Dion /1988 / Switzerland

Sandie Shaw / 1967 / United Kingdom

Brotherhood of Man / 1976 / United Kingdom

ABBA / 1974 / Sweden

Johnny Logan /1980 / Ireland

THE SEVEN WONDERS OF THE ANCIENT WORLD

The Colossus of Rhodes

The Great Pyramids of Giza (still standing today in Egypt)

The Hanging Gardens of Babylon

The Lighthouse of Alexandria

The Mausoleum of Halicarnassus

The Statue of Zeus at Olympia

The Temple of Artemis

METRIC AND IMPERIAL

Imperial	Metric
1 inch	2.54 cm
1 mile	1.61 km
1 hectare	10 000m²
1 pint	0.57 litres
1 stone	6.35 kg
1 long ton	1.02 tonnes

THE SYMPHONY ORCHESTRA

Strings

Violins (First and Second)
Violas
Cellos
Double Basses
Harp

Woodwind

Flutes
Oboes
Clarinets
Bassoons

Brass

Horns
Trumpets
Trombones
Tuba

Percussion

Timpani
Bass Drum
Snare Drum
Cymbals

THE JAMES BOND FILMS

The Sean Connery Movies

1962	*Dr. No*
1963	*From Russia With Love*
1964	*Goldfinger*
1965	*Thunderball*
1967	*You Only Live Twice*
1971	*Diamonds Are Forever*
1983	*Never Say Never Again*

The George Lazenby Movie

| 1969 | *On Her Majesty's Secret Service* |

The Roger Moore Movies

1973	*Live and Let Die*
1974	*The Man With the Golden Gun*
1977	*The Spy Who Loved Me*
1979	*Moonraker*
1981	*For Your Eyes Only*
1983	*Octopussy*
1985	*A View to a Kill*

The Timothy Dalton Movies

1987 *The Living Daylights*

1989 *Licence to Kill*

The Pierce Brosnan Movies

1995 *GoldenEye*

1997 *Tomorrow Never Dies*

1999 *The World is Not Enough*

2002 *Die Another Day*

The Daniel Craig Movies

2006 *Casino Royale*

2008 *Quantum of Solace*

SNOOKER LOOPY

Red

Yellow

Green

Brown

Blue

Pink

Black

INTERNATIONAL CURRENCIES

Venezuela

Costa Rica and El Salvador

Morocco and the United Arab
   Emirates

Vietnam

Hungary

Ukraine

The Czech Republic

Angola

Albania

Swaziland

Nigeria

Bhutan

Guatemala

Brazil

Malaysia

Russia and Belarus

Israel

Japan

China

Poland

SHAKESPEARE'S PLAYS

Histories

Henry IV, part I

Henry IV, part II

Henry V

Henry VI, part I

Henry VI, part II

Henry VI, part III

Henry VIII

King John

Richard II

Richard III

Tragedies

Antony and Cleopatra

Coriolanus

Cymbeline

Hamlet

Julius Caesar

King Lear

Macbeth

Othello

Romeo and Juliet

Timon of Athens

Titus Andronicus

Troilus and Cressida

Comedies

A Midsummer Night's Dream

All's Well That Ends Well

As You Like It

The Comedy of Errors

Love's Labour's Lost

Measure for Measure

The Merchant of Venice

The Merry Wives of Windsor

Much Ado About Nothing

Pericles, Prince of Tyre

The Taming of the Shrew

The Tempest

The Two Gentlemen of Verona

The Winter's Tale

Twelfth Night or *What You Will*

THE LONDON UNDERGROUND

A Edgware Road

B Baker Street

C Great Portland Street

D Euston Square

E King's Cross St Pancras

F Farringdon

G Barbican

H Moorgate

I Liverpool Street

J Aldgate

K Tower Hill

L Monument

M Cannon Street

N Mansion House

O Blackfriars

P Temple

Q Embankment

R Westminster

S St James's Park

T Victoria

U Sloane Square

V South Kensington

W Gloucester Road

X High Street Kensington

Y Notting Hill Gate

Z Bayswater

SNOW WHITE'S DWARFS

Bashful

Doc

Dopey

Grumpy

Happy

Sleepy

Sneezy

MIXING IT UP

Bloody Mary

Singapore Sling

Long Island Ice Tea

Mojito

Margarita

Cosmopolitan

Harvey Wallbanger

Screwdriver

White Russian

Manhattan

THE GREEK ALPHABET

Alpha

Beta

Gamma

Delta

Epsilon

Zeta

Eta

Theta

Iota

Kappa

Lambda

Mu

Nu

Xi

Omicron

Pi

Rho

Sigma

Tau

Upsilon

Phi

Chi

Psi

Omega

CHAMPAGNE CHARLIE

Magnum

Jeroboam

Rehoboam

Methuselah

Salmanazar

Balthazar

Nebuchadnezzar

US STATES AND THEIR CAPITALS

State	Capital
Alabama	Montgomery
Alaska	Juneau
Arizona	Phoenix
Arkansas	Little Rock
California	Sacramento
Colorado	Denver
Connecticut	Hartford
Delaware	Dover
Florida	Tallahassee
Georgia	Atlanta
Hawaii	Honolulu
Idaho	Boise
Illinois	Springfield
Indiana	Indianapolis
Iowa	Des Moines
Kansas	Topeka
Kentucky	Frankfort
Louisiana	Baton Rouge
Maine	Augusta
Maryland	Annapolis
Massachusetts	Boston
Michigan	Lansing
Minnesota	St Paul
Mississippi	Jackson
Missouri	Jefferson City
Montana	Helena
Nebraska	Lincoln
Nevada	Carson City
New Hampshire	Concord
New Jersey	Trenton
New Mexico	Santa Fe
New York	Albany
North Carolina	Raleigh
North Dakota	Bismarck
Ohio	Columbus
Oklahoma	Oklahoma City
Oregon	Salem
Pennsylvania	Harrisburg
Rhode Island	Providence
South Carolina	Columbia
South Dakota	Pierre
Tennessee	Nashville
Texas	Austin
Utah	Salt Lake City
Vermont	Montpelier
Virginia	Richmond
Washington	Olympia
West Virginia	Charleston
Wisconsin	Madison
Wyoming	Cheyenne

GREAT FILM TAGLINES

King Kong

Pinocchio

The Red Shoes

Singin' in the Rain

Rebel Without a Cause
Psycho
The Sound of Music
A Clockwork Orange
Jaws
Taxi Driver
Star Wars
Superman: The Movie
Alien
Ghostbusters
Back to the Future
Platoon
A Fish Called Wanda
When Harry Met Sally
The Silence of the Lambs
Groundhog Day
The Shawshank Redemption
Fargo
The Matrix
Shrek
Lost in Translation

Toronto, Canada
Urubamba Valley, Peru
Moscow, Russia
Beijing, China
Kyoto, Japan
Barcelona, Spain
Northern Territory, Australia
South Dakota, USA
Agra, India
Istanbul, Turkey
Copenhagen, Denmark
Vienna, Austria
Athens, Greece

TYPES OF TREE

A Alder
B Common Ash
C Labernum
D Common Oak
E Rowan
F Palm
G Silver Birch
H Yew
I Sycamore
J Monkey Puzzle
K Common Beech
L English Elm
M Holly
N Scots Pine
O Weeping Willow
P Redwood

WORLD LANDMARKS

Rome, Italy
Budapest, Hungary
Dubai, UAE
Rio de Janeiro, Brazil
Split, Croatia
Mostar, Bosnia and Herzegovina
Aswan, Egypt

Q Norway Spruce

R Linden

S Horse Chestnut

T Copper Beech

THE SIGNS OF THE ZODIAC

Aries

Taurus

Gemini

Cancer

Leo

Virgo

Libra

Scorpio

Sagittarius

Capricorn

Aquarius

Pisces

SCRABBLE TILES

A, E, I, L, N, O, R, S, T, U

D, G

B, C, M, P

F, H, V, W, Y

K

J, X

Q, Z

THE OSCARS: THE BIGGEST WINNERS

Titanic

Ben-Hur

The Lord of the Rings: The Return of the King

West Side Story

The English Patient

Gigi

The Last Emperor

Gone With the Wind

From Here to Eternity

On the Waterfront

My Fair Lady

Gandhi

Amadeus

Cabaret

Slumdog Millionaire

Shakespeare in Love

Dances With Wolves

Schindler's List

Out of Africa

Going My Way

Lawrence of Arabia

Patton

The Sting

The Best Years of Our Lives

The Bridge on the River Kwai

GREAT ARTISTS

Henri Matisse

Rembrandt van Rijn

Pablo Picasso

Raphael

Paul Cézanne

Edvard Munch

Claude Monet

Vincent van Gogh

Salvador Dalí

Leonardo da Vinci

Caravaggio

Wassily Kandinsky

Gustav Klimt

René Magritte

Andy Warhol

Frida Kahlo

Edgar Degas

Pierre-Auguste Renoir

Michelangelo Buonarotti

Titian

SONGS FROM THE MUSICALS

Carousel

Oklahoma!

Annie Get Your Gun

Show Boat

Porgy and Bess

Guys and Dolls

Grease

High Society

The King and I

Kiss Me, Kate

Mary Poppins

My Fair Lady

Oliver!

The Phantom of the Opera

Rent

The Rocky Horror Show

South Pacific

The Sound of Music

West Side Story

Les Misérables

THE HUMAN SKELETON

A Cranial bones/skull

B Mandible

C Clavicle (collarbone)

D Scapula (shoulder blade)

E Sternum (breastbone)

F Ribcage

G Ribs

H Humerus

I Spinal column

J Radius

K Ulna

L Pelvis

M Ossa coxae (hip bones)

N Sacrum

O Coccyx (tail bone)

P Carpal (wrist)

Q Metacarpal bones

R Phalanges (finger bones)

S Femur

T Patella (kneecap)

U Tibia

V Fibula

W Tarsal bones

X Metatarsal bones

Y Phalanges (toes)

THE SAFARI 'BIG FIVE'

Lion

Leopard

Black Rhino

Elephant

Cape Buffalo

THE MODERN DECATHLON

100m Sprint

Long Jump

Shot Put

High Jump

400m Sprint

110m Hurdles

Discus

Pole Vault

Javelin

1500m Sprint

THE WORLD'S LONGEST RIVERS

Nile (Africa)

Amazon (South America)

Yangtze (Asia)

Mississippi-Missouri System (North America)

Ob'-Irtysh (Asia)

Yenisey-Angara (Asia)

Huang He (Yellow) (Asia)

Congo (Africa)

THE PERIODIC TABLE

A

Hydrogen

Helium

Lithium

Beryllium

Boron

Carbon

Nitrogen

Oxygen

B

Helium

Neon

Argon

Krypton

Xenon

Radon

C

Sodium

Magnesium

Potassium

Titanium

Arsenic

Rhodium

Tin

Tungsten

Gold

Plutonium

Rutherfordium

**WHAT THE ROMANS
DID FOR US**

magnum opus

quid pro quo

habeas corpus

ad hoc

in flagrante delicto

caveat emptor

in vitro

vice versa

Alma Mater

modus operandi

GREAT POEMS

'Jabberwocky',
    Lewis Carroll

'Ozymandias',
    Percy Bysshe Shelley

'Remember',
    Christina Rossetti

'Sonnet 43',
    Elizabeth Barrett Browning

'Auld Lang Syne',
    Robert Burns

'The Whitsun Weddings',
    Philip Larkin

'Anthem for Doomed Youth',
    Wilfred Owen

'To Autumn',
    John Keats

'Skimbleshanks: The
    Railway Cat', T. S. Eliot

'The Charge of the Light
    Brigade', Alfred Lord
    Tennyson

'If', Rudyard Kipling

'Funeral Blues', W. H. Auden

'The Raven',
    Edgar Allan Poe

'Composed upon Westminster
    Bridge, September 3, 1802',
    William Wordsworth
'Sonnet XVIII',
    William Shakespeare

THE HITS OF ELVIS

'(Let Me Be Your) Teddy Bear'
'(Marie's The Name) His
    Latest Flame'
'(Now And Then There's)
    A Fool Such As I'
'(You're The) Devil In Disguise'
'A Big Hunk O' Love'
'A Little Less Conversation'
    (JXL Remix)
'All Shook Up'
'Are You Lonesome Tonight?'
'Burning Love'
'Can't Help Falling In Love'
'Crying In The Chapel'
'Don't'
'Don't Be Cruel'
'Good Luck Charm'
'Hard Headed Woman'
'Heartbreak Hotel'
'Hound Dog'
'In The Ghetto'
'It's Now Or Never'
'Jailhouse Rock'

'Love Me Tender'
'One Night'
'Return To Sender'
'She's Not You'
'Stuck On You'
'Surrender'
'Suspicious Minds'
'The Wonder Of You'
'Too Much'
'Way Down'
'Wooden Heart'

NOMS DE PLUME

Acton Bell
Doctor Seuss
George Eliot
George Orwell
John le Carré
Joseph Conrad
Lewis Carroll
Mark Twain
Tennessee Williams
Tom Stoppard

US MILITARY RANKS

Private

Private 2

Private First Class

Specialist

Corporal

Sergeant

Staff Sergeant

Sergeant First Class

Master Sergeant

First Sergeant

Sergeant Major

Command Sergeant Major

Sergeant Major of the Army

Warrant Officer

Chief Warrant Officer 2

Chief Warrant Officer 3

Chief Warrant Officer 4

Chief Warrant Officer 5

Second Lieutenant

First Lieutenant

Captain

Major

Lieutenant Colonel

Colonel

Brigadier General

Major General

Lieutenant General

General

General of the Army

WHO'S THE ACTOR?

William Hartnell

Patrick Troughton

Jon Pertwee

Tom Baker

Peter Davison

Colin Baker

Sylvester McCoy

Paul McGann

Christopher Eccleston

David Tennant

Matt Smith

(and Richard Hurndall in
The Five Doctors)

GREAT INVENTIONS

Lazlo Biro

Trevor Baylis

John Pemberton

Alfred Nobel

Clarence Birdseye

Joseph and Jacques Montgolfier

Frank Whittle

Richard Gatling

Willhelm Schickard

Percy Spencer

Thomas A. Edison

Johannes Gutenberg

James Hargreaves

René Laënnec

Alexander Graham Bell

BOOKS OF THE NEW TESTAMENT

Matthew

Mark

Luke

John

Acts

Romans

I Corinthians

II Corinthians

Galatians

Ephesians

Philippians

Colossians

I Thessalonians

II Thessalonians

I Timothy

II Timothy

Titus

Philemon

Hebrews

James

I Peter

II Peter

I John

II John

III John

Jude

Revelation

BIRTHSTONES

Jan   Garnet or Rose Quartz

Feb   Amethyst or Onyx

Mar Bloodstone or Aquamarine

Apr   Diamond or Rock Crystal

May Emerald or Chrysoprase

Jun   Pearl or Moonstone

Jul   Ruby or Carnelion

Aug Peridot or Sardonyx

Sept Sapphire or Lapis

Oct   Opal or Tourmaline

Nov Topaz or Citrine

Dec   Tanzanite, Zircon or
      Turquoise

NEW NATIONS

Croatia

Slovenia

The Marshall Islands

Micronesia

Bosnia and Herzegovina

Serbia and Montenegro

The Czech Republic

Eritrea

Macedonia

Slovakia

Palau

East Timor

FAMOUS DATES
IN HISTORY

753 BC

560 BC

AD 312

AD 570

AD 1215

AD 1492

AD 1776

AD 1789

AD 1815

AD 1859

AD 1916

AD 1917

AD 1945

AD 1959

AD 1989

THE MORSE
THE MERRIER

A .-

B -...

C -.-.

D -..

E .

F ..-.

G --.

H ....

I ..

J .---

K -.-

L .-..

M --

N -.

O ---

P .--.

Q --.-

R .-.

S ...

T -

U ..-

V ...-

W .--

X -..-

Y -.--

Z --..

WHICH TROPHY,
WHICH SPORT?

Rugby Union

Ice hockey

Yacht racing

Basketball

American football

Women's tennis

Golf

Cycling

Horse racing

Badminton

THE SUMMER OLYMPICS

Athens (Greece)

Paris (France)

St. Louis (USA)

London (UK)

Stockholm (Sweden)

Antwerp (Belgium)

Paris (France)

Amsterdam (Netherlands)

Los Angeles (USA)

Berlin (Germany)

London (UK)

Helsinki (Finland)

Melbourne (Australia)

Rome (Italy)

Tokyo (Japan)

Mexico City (Mexico)

Munich (Germany)

Montreal (Canada)

Moscow (USSR)

Los Angeles (USA)

Seoul (South Korea)

Barcelona (Spain)

Atlanta (USA)

Sydney (Australia)

Athens (Greece)

Beijing (China)

London (UK)

Rio de Janeiro (Brazil)

FRENCH WINE REGIONS

A Alsace

B Bordeaux

C Burgundy

D Champagne

E Corsica

F Cotes du Rhone

G Languedoc-Roussillon

H Loire Valley

I Provence

J South West

KINGS AND QUEENS OF ENGLAND AND BRITAIN

Charles II

James II

William III

Queen Mary II

Queen Anne

George I

George II

George III

George IV

William IV

Victoria

Edward VII

George V

Edward VIII

George VI

Elizabeth II

THE WORLD'S HIGHEST MOUNTAINS

Mount Everest

Aconcagua

Mount McKinley

Mount Kilimanjaro

Mount Elbrus

Vinson Massif

Mount Kosciusko

A STAR IS BORN

Meat Loaf

Fred Astaire

Axl Rose

Marilyn Monroe

Tina Turner

Elton John

Shania Twain

Chubby Checker

Alice Cooper

Judy Garland

Patsy Cline

Bono

Whoopi Goldberg

Stevie Wonder

Woody Allen

Cher

Cary Grant

John Wayne

George Michael

Lauren Bacall

Tony Curtis

Sting

Marilyn Manson

Julie Andrews

Bob Dylan

BEST ACTOR OSCARS

Fredric March

Spencer Tracy

Gary Cooper

Marlon Brando

Jack Nicholson

Dustin Hoffman

Daniel Day-Lewis

Tom Hanks

Sean Penn

BEST ACTRESS OSCARS

Katharine Hepburn

Bette Davis

Luise Rainer

Vivien Leigh

Ingrid Bergman

Olivia de Havilland

Elizabeth Taylor

Glenda Jackson

Jane Fonda

Sally Field

Jodie Foster

Hilary Swank

HOW MANY PLAYERS?

11

15

13

11

6

4

5

9

11

11

18

10

12

INTERNATIONAL ORGANIZATIONS ACRONYMS

European Free Trade Association

Food and Agriculture Organization

International Atomic Energy Agency

International Bank for Reconstruction and Development (The World Bank)

International Committee of The Red Cross

International Monetary Fund

International Olympic Committee

North Atlantic Treaty Organization

Organization for Economic Co-Operation and Development

Organization of the Petroleum Exporting Countries

United Nations

United Nations Educational, Scientific and Cultural Organization

World Health Organization

World Intellectual Property Organization

World Trade Organization

THE CHRONICLES OF NARNIA

The Lion, the Witch and the Wardrobe

Prince Caspian: The Return to Narnia

The Voyage of the Dawn Treader

The Silver Chair

The Horse and His Boy

The Magician's Nephew

The Last Battle

ANIMAL COLLECTIVE NOUNS

Hyenas

Finches

Bats

Cockroaches

Toads

Moles

Crows

Owls

Locusts

Dolphins

Lions

Apes

Jellyfish

Tigers

Ravens

AUSTRALIA'S STATES AND TERRITORIES

A   Australian Capital Territory

B   New South Wales

C   Northern Territory

D   Queensland

E   South Australia

F   Tasmania

G   Victoria

H   Western Australia

COASTLINES

Canada

Indonesia

Russia

Philippines

Japan

Australia

Norway

USA

New Zealand

China

ANIMAL YOUNG

Kit

Fawn

Nymph

Kid

Gosling

Joey
Cygnet
Elver
Leveret
Owlet

Golf
The Masters
US Open
The Open Championship/
    British Open
US PGA Championship

ANNIVERSARIES
Paper
Cotton
Leather
Wood
Tin/Aluminum
Crystal
China
Silver
Pearl
Jade/Coral
Ruby
Sapphire
Gold
Emerald
Diamond

THE BOOKS OF ROALD DAHL
James and the Giant Peach
Danny, the Champion of the
    World
The Vicar of Nibbleswicke
George's Marvellous Medicine
The Gremlins
The Minpins
The BFG
The Witches
Charlie and the Chocolate Factory
Charlie and the Great Glass
    Elevator
Matilda
Fantastic Mr Fox

GRAND SLAMS
Tennis
Australian Open
French Open
Wimbledon
US Open

WORLD'S LONGEST MOUNTAIN RANGES
Andes (South America)
Rocky Mountains (North
    America)

Himalaya-Karakoram-Hindu
  Kush (Asia)

Great Dividing Range
  (Australia)

Trans-Antarctic Mountains
  (Antarctica)

THE TWELVE DISCIPLES

Andrew

Bartholomew

James

James the Younger

John

Judas Iscariot

Matthew

Philip

Simon Peter

Simon the Zealot

Thaddaeus, also known as
  'Judas, son of James'

Thomas

COMPLETE THE PROVERBS

A little **learning/knowledge**
  is a dangerous thing.

Beware of **Greeks** bearing
  gifts.

Don't count your **chickens**
  before they've **hatched**.

Let sleeping **dogs** lie.

Never judge a **book** by its **cover**.

Revenge is a **dish** best served
  cold.

You can't make a **silk purse**
  from a **sow's ear**.

A **fool** and his **money** are
  soon parted.

Beauty is in the eye of the
  beholder.

Discretion is the better part
  of **valour**.

It's the early **bird** that gets
  the **worm**.

Mighty **oaks** from little
  acorns grow.

People who live in **glass houses**
  shouldn't throw **stones**.

Too many **cooks** spoil the
  broth.

Absence makes the **heart**
  grow fonder.

Cleanliness is next to godliness.

Don't upset the **apple cart**.

Make **hay** while the sun **shines**.

One man's **meat** is another
  man's **poison**.

Tell the **truth** and shame
  the **Devil**.

IF YOU WANT TO GET AHEAD...

A Bowler

B Cloche

C Fedora

D Fez

E Panama

F Porkpie

G Top Hat

H Trilby

I Kufi

J Straw Boater

K Tam o'shanter

L Deerstalker

M Homburg

N Sombrero

THE WINTER OLYMPICS

Chamonix, France

St. Moritz, Switzerland

Lake Placid, New York, USA

Garmisch-Partenkirchen, Germany

St. Moritz, Switzerland

Oslo, Norway

Cortina d'Ampezzo, Italy

Squaw Valley, California, USA

Innsbruck, Austria

Grenoble, France

Sapporo, Japan

Innsbruck, Austria

Lake Placid, New York, USA

Sarajevo, Yugoslavia

Calgary, Canada

Albertville, France

Lillehammer, Norway

Nagano, Japan

Salt Lake City, USA

Turin, Italy

Vancouver, Canada

Sochi, Russia

CANADIAN PROVINCES AND TERRITORIES

A Ontario

B British Colombia

C Alberta

D Manitoba

E Quebec

F Yukon

G Northwest Territories

H Saskatchewan

I Nova Scotia

J New Brunswick

K Prince Edward Island

L Newfoundland

M Nunavut

GREAT ARCHITECTS AND THEIR BUILDINGS

Andrea Palladio

James Hoban

Jørn Utzon

Christopher Wren

Frank Lloyd Wright

Antoni Gaudí

Gian Lorenzo Bernini

Le Corbusier

Edwin Lutyens

Charles Rennie Mackintosh

Filippo Brunelleschi

William Van Alen

Walter Gropius

Inigo Jones

Norman Foster

THE CHARACTERS OF ENID BLYTON

Famous Five

Anne

Dick

George

Julian

Timmy the Dog

Secret Seven

Barbara

Colin

George

Jack

Janet

Pam

Peter

BASEBALL THE WORLD SERIES

New York Yankees

St. Louis Cardinals

Oakland Athletics

Boston Red Sox

Los Angeles Dodgers

New York Giants

Cincinnati Reds

Pittsburgh Pirates

THE CANTERBURY TALES

'The Knight'

'The Miller'

'The Reeve'

'The Cook'

'The Man of Law'

'The Wife of Bath'

'The Friar'

'The Summoner'

'The Clerk'

'The Merchant'

'The Squire'
'The Franklin'
'The Physician'
'The Pardoner'
'The Shipman'
'The Prioress'
'Sir Thopas'
'Melibee'
'The Monk'
'The Nun'
'The Second Nun'
'The Canon's Yeoman'
'The Manciple'
'The Parson'

Glaswegian
Tapatío
Saigonese
Vegan
Liverpudlian
Capitalino
Muscovite
Münchner
Neapolitan
Sydneysider

RUGBY WORLD CUP
New Zealand
Australia
South Africa
Australia
England
South Africa

DEMONYMS
Bolognese
Cantabrigian
Capetonian
Caraquenian
Florentine

THE COMPLETE WORKS OF GILBERT AND SULLIVAN

Thespis (1871)
Trial by Jury (1875)
The Sorcerer (1877)
HMS Pinafore (1878)
The Pirates of Penzance (1879)
Patience (1881)
Iolanthe (1882)
Princess Ida (1884)
The Mikado (1885)
Ruddigore (1887)
The Yeoman of the Guard (1888)
The Gondoliers (1889)
Utopia Ltd (1893)
The Grand Duke (1896)

TYPES OF CLOUD

High clouds
Cirrus

Cirrocumulus

Cirrostratus

Medium clouds
Altocumulus

Altostratus

Nimbostratus

Low clouds
Stratocumulus

Stratus

Cumulus

Cumulonimbus

WIMBLEDON TENNIS CHAMPIONS

Men's
Pete Sampras

Roger Federer

Bjorn Borg

Boris Becker

John McEnroe

Jimmy Connors

Stefan Edberg

Rod Laver

John Newcombe

Ladies'
Martina Navratilova

Steffi Graf

Venus Williams

Billie Jean King

Chris Evert

Serena Williams

INDIAN STATES

States
Andhra Pradesh

Arunachal Pradesh

Assam

Bihar

Chhattisgarh

Goa

Gujarat

Haryana

Himachal Pradesh

Jammu and Kashmir

Jharkhand

Karnataka

Kerala

Madhya Pradesh

Maharashtra

Manipur

Meghalaya

Mizoram

Nagaland

Orissa

Punjab

Rajasthan

Sikkim

Tamil Nadu

Tripura

Uttar Pradesh

Uttarakhand

West Bengal

Union Territories

Andaman and Nicobar Islands

Chandigarh

Dadra and Nagar Haveli

Daman and Diu

Delhi

Lakshadweep

Puducherry

COMPUTING ACRONYMS

Asymmetric Digital Subscriber
  Line

Basic Input/Output System

Bitmap

Compact Disc Read-Only
  Memory

Central Processing Unit

Disk Operating System

Dots Per Inch

Document Type Definition

Garbage In, Garbage Out

Global Positioning System

Hyper-Text Markup Language

Hyper-Text Transfer Protocol

Instant Message

Internet Service Provider

Joint Photographic Experts
  Group

Megabits Per Second

Portable Document Format

Uniform Resource Locator

Universal Serial Bus

World Wide Web

THE NOVELS OF CHARLES DICKENS

David Copperfield

Oliver Twist

A Christmas Carol

Martin Chuzzlewit

A Tale of Two Cities

Great Expectations

The Pickwick Papers

Nicholas Nickleby

The Old Curiosity Shop

Barnaby Rudge

Dombey and Son

Bleak House

Hard Times

Little Dorrit

Our Mutual Friend

The Mystery of Edwin Drood

THE SIX WIVES OF HENRY VIII

Catherine of Aragon

Anne Boleyn

Jane Seymour

Anne of Cleves

Kathryn Howard

Katherine Parr

ROMAN NUMERALS

I

V

X

L

C

D

M

MCDXXXV

(1459 − 24 = 1435)

GODS OF GREEK AND ROMAN MYTHOLOGY

Greek	Roman
Zeus	Jupiter
Poseidon	Neptune
Hades	Pluto
Hestia	Vesta
Ares	Mars
Athena	Minerva
Apollo	Apollo
Aphrodite	Venus
Hermes	Mercury
Artemis	Diana
Hephaestus	Vulcan
Dionysus	Bacchus
Eros	Cupid
Hypnos	Somnus

THE CREW OF THE USS ENTERPRISE IN THE ORIGINAL STAR TREK

Role / Actor

James T. Kirk / William Shatner

Spock / Leonard Nimoy

Leonard 'Bones' McCoy /
   DeForest Kelley

Montgomery 'Scotty' Scott /
   James Doohan

Nyota Uhura / Nichelle Nichols

Hikaru Sulu / George Takei

Pavel Chekov / Walter Koenig

Janice Rand / Grace Lee
   Whitney

Christine Chapel / Majel Barrett

CAPITAL CITIES OF ASIA

Kabul

Baku

Dhaka

Thimphu

Phnom Penh

Beijing

New Delhi

Jakarta

Tokyo

P'yongyang

Seoul

Kuala Lumpur

Ulan Bator

Kathmandu

Islamabad

Manila

Bangkok

Ashgabat

Tashkent

Hanoi

MUSICAL NOTATION

A   Treble clef

B   Bass clef

C   Semibreve

D   Minim

E   Crotchet

F   Quaver

G   Semiquaver

THE FELLOWSHIP OF THE LORD OF THE RINGS

Gimli

Legolas

Frodo Baggins

Meriadoc Brandybuck (Merry)

Peregrin Took (Pippin)

Samwise Gamgee (Sam)

Aragorn (Strider)

Boromir

Gandalf the Grey

BROTHERS AND SISTERS

Marx Brothers

Chico

Harpo

Groucho

Gummo

Zeppo

Gibbs (The BeeGees)

Barry

Robin

Maurice

Andrews Sisters

LaVerne

Maxene

Patty

Beverley Sisters
Joy
Teddie
Babs

Osmonds
Donny
Marie
Alan
Wayne
Merrill
Jay
Jimmy

Jonas Brothers
Kevin
Joe
Nick

THE EARTH'S ATMOSPHERE
Troposphere
Stratosphere
Mesosphere
Thermosphere
Exosphere

DINOSAURS
Diplodocus
Oviraptor
Triceratops
Ichthyosaurus
Iguanodon
Stegosaurus
Velociraptor
Allosaurus
Tyrannosaurus Rex
Pteradactyl

ROYAL HOUSES
Bahrain
Belgium
Bhutan
Denmark and Norway
United Kingdom
Monaco
Morocco
Netherlands
Saudi Arabia
Luxembourg and Spain
Swaziland
Sweden
Thailand
Tonga

TYPE-CAST
QWERTYUIOP
ASDFGHJKL
ZXCVBNM

Goat
Monkey
Rooster
Dog
Boar

INTERNATIONAL TIME ZONES

-09:00 hours
+12:00 hours
+08:00 hours
-10:00 hours
+03:00 hours
+05:30 hours
-05:00 hours
+01:00 hours
+02:00 hours
-05:00 hours
+10:00 hours
+09:00 hours

ISO CODES

Austria
Australia
Bosnia and Herzegovina
Burkina Faso
China
Czech Republic
Germany
Estonia
Spain
Croatia
Ireland
Mexico
Netherlands
Poland
Qatar
Sweden
Chad
Holy See (Vatican City State)
South Africa
Zambia

CHINESE ANIMAL ZODIAC

Rat
Ox
Tiger
Rabbit
Dragon
Snake
Horse

I AM, YOU ARE, HE IS…

French

Etre…

Je suis

Tu es

Il/elle/on est

Nous sommes

Vous êtes

Ils/elles sont

German

Sein…

Ich bin

Du bist

Er/sie/es ist

Wir sind

Ihr seid

Sie sind

Italian

Essere…

Io sono

Tu sei

Lui/lei/Lei è

Noi siamo

Voi siete

Loro sono

Spanish

Ser/Estar

Yo soy/estoy

Tú eres/estás

Él/ella/usted es/está

Nosotros somos/estamos

Vosotros sois/estáis

Ellos/ellas/ustedes son/están

THE NOVELS OF THE BRONTË SISTERS

Anne

Pen Name: Acton Bell

Novels: *Agnes Grey; The Tenant of Wildfell Hall*

Charlotte

Pen Name: Currer Bell

Novels: *The Green Dwarf; Tales of Angria; Jane Eyre; Shirley; Villette; The Professor*

Emily

Pen Name: Ellis Bell

Novel: *Wuthering Heights*

WHO WAS ON DRUMS?

The Beatles

John Lennon

Paul McCartney

George Harrison

Ringo Starr

Fleetwood Mac
Lindsey Buckingham
Mick Fleetwood
John McVie
Stevie Nicks

Abba
Benny Andersson
Agnetha Fältskog
Anni-Frid Lyngstad
Björn Ulvaeus

The Jackson 5
Jackie
Jermaine (later replaced
  by Randy)
Marlon
Michael
Tito

U2
Bono
The Edge
Adam Clayton
Larry Mullen, Jr

The Monkees
Michael Nesmith
Davy Jones
Micky Dolenz
Peter Tork

Queen
John Deacon
Brian May
Freddie Mercury
Roger Taylor

THE MOON'S SEAS
Ocean of Storms
Sea of Cold
Sea of Showers or Sea of Rains
Sea of Fertility
Sea of Tranquility
Sea of Clouds
Sea of Serenity
Southern Sea
Sea of Islands

THE G7
Canada
France
Germany
Italy
Japan
USA
UK

THE MONOPOLY BOARD

US Edition / UK Edition

Mediterranean Avenue /
Old Kent Road

Baltic Avenue /
Whitechapel Road

Oriental Avenue /
The Angel Islington

Vermont Avenue / Euston Road

Connecticut / Pentonville Road

St. Charles Place / Pall Mall

States Avenue / Whitehall

Virginia Avenue /
Northumberland Avenue

St. James Place / Bow Street

Tennessee Avenue /
Marlborough Street

New York Avenue / Vine Street

Kentucky Avenue / Strand

Indiana Avenue / Fleet Street

Illinois Avenue / Trafalgar
Square

Atlantic Avenue / Leicester
Square

Ventnor Avenue / Coventry
Street

Marvin Gardens / Piccadilly

Pacific Avenue / Regent Street

North Carolina Avenue /
Oxford Street

Pennsylvania Avenue /
Bond Street

Park Place / Park Lane

Boardwalk / Mayfair

SEMAPHORE SIGNALS

Pack my box with five dozen
liquor jugs.

(*A sentence using all twenty-six
letters of the alphabet.*)

LANDLOCKED NATIONS

Paraguay

Rwanda

Laos

Ethiopia

Armenia

Austria

Vatican City

Kazakhstan

Hungary

Zimbabwe

WORLD'S LARGEST COUNTRIES

Russia
Canada
USA
China
Brazil
Australia
India
Argentina
Kazakhstan
Sudan

DAYS OF THE WEEK IN DIFFERENT LANGUAGES

French / German / Spanish / Italian

Lundi / Montag / lunes / lunedì
Mardi / Dienstag / martes / martedì
Mercredi / Mittwoch /miércoles / mercoledì
Jeudi / Donnerstag / jueves / giovedì
Vendredi / Freitag /viernes / venerdì
Samedi / Samstag /sábado / sabato
Dimanche / Sonntag / domingo / domenica

UNITED NATIONS SECRETARY GENERALS

Name / Nationality
Trygve Lie / Norway
Dag Hammarskjöld / Sweden
U Thant / Myanmar
Kurt Waldheim / Austria
Javier Pérez de Cuéllar / Peru
Boutros Boutros-Ghali / Egypt
Kofi Annan / Ghana
Ban Ki-moon / South Korea

CHESS PIECES

King
Queen
Bishops
Knights
Rooks
Pawns

WHO SAID WHAT? (PART I)

Martin Luther King, Jr.
Abraham Lincoln
Albert Einstein
Mark Twain
Aristotle
Mahatma Gandhi
George Bernard Shaw

Winston Churchill
Mother Teresa
John Lennon

MUSICAL TERMS
Grave
Largo
Adagio
Andante
Allegro
Vivace
Presto
Moderato
Accelerando
Ritardando

THE HEPTATHLON
100m hurdles
High jump
Shot put
200m sprint
Long jump
Javelin
800m sprint

INTERNATIONAL AIRPORT CODES
Stockholm (Arlanda)
Brisbane
Mumbai (Chhatrapati Shivaji)
Paris (Charles De Gaulle)
Dubai
Guadalajara (Don Miguel Hidalgo y Costilla)
Rio de Janeiro (Galeão–Antonio Carlos Jobim)
New York (John F. Kennedy International)
Los Angeles International
London (Heathrow)
Lagos (Murtala Muhammed)
Tokyo (Narita)
Moscow (Sheremetyevo)
Berlin (Tegel 'Otto Lilienthal')
Vancouver

PUTTING A NAME TO A DISH
Giuseppe Garibaldi (Garibaldi biscuit)
Charles Grey, Viscount Howick (Earl Grey tea)
Margherita of Savoy (margherita)

Dame Nellie Melba
(peach melba)
Anna Pavlova (pavlova)
John Montagu, 4th Earl
of Sandwich (sandwich)
Edward VII (King Edward
potato)
Arthur Wellesley, Duke of
Wellington (Beef Wellington)
Frederick Marquis, Earl of
Woolton (Woolton Pie)

DISNEY FEATURE FILMS

*Snow White and the Seven
Dwarfs*
Pinocchio
Fantasia
Dumbo
Bambi
Saludos Amigos
The Three Caballeros
Make Mine Music
Fun and Fancy Free
Melody Time
*The Adventures of Ichabod
and Mr. Toad*
Cinderella
Alice in Wonderland
Peter Pan

Lady and the Tramp
Sleeping Beauty
*One Hundred and One
Dalmatians*
The Sword in the Stone
The Jungle Book

WHO LIVES THERE?

Prime Minister of the UK
The Addams Family
Lord Peter Wimsey
Miss Marple
The drinkers of the bar in *Cheers*
Michael Jackson
White House, US President
of the USA
Clark Kent and Lois Lane
Sherlock Holmes
Dr Dolittle
Tony Hancock (*Hancock's
Half Hour*)
Paddington Bear
Ewing family (*Dallas*)
Harry Potter
Clampett family (*Beverly
Hillbillies*)
Cunningham Family
(*Happy Days*)
Batman
Wallace and Gromit

Jessica Fletcher (*Murder,
    She Wrote*)

The Simpsons

OLOGIES

Humankind

Spiders

Bell ringing

The heart

Mollusc shells

Skin

The Earth

Ageing

Blood

Weather

Clouds

Cancer

Eggs

Eyes

Birds

Bones

Prehistoric creatures

Drugs

Earthquakes

Flags

**HITS OF
THE BEATLES**

'A Hard Day's Night'

'All You Need Is Love'

'Can't Buy Me Love'

'Come Together'

'Day Tripper'

'Eight Days A Week'

'Eleanor Rigby'

'From Me To You'

'Get Back'

'Hello, Goodbye'

'Help!'

'Hey Jude'

'I Feel Fine'

'I Want To Hold Your Hand'

'Lady Madonna'

'Let It Be'

'Love Me Do'

'Paperback Writer'

'Penny Lane'

'She Loves You'

'Something'

'The Ballad Of John And Yoko'

'The Long And Winding Road'

'Ticket To Ride'

'We Can Work It Out'

'Yellow Submarine'

'Yesterday'

1+1=2

Butt-Head
Bob Hope
Lou Costello
Tommy Chong
Jerry Lewis
Peter Cook
Eric Morecambe
Fred Astaire
George Burns
Tina Turner
Dianne Lee
Teller
Renato
Cher
Hugh Laurie

AFRICAN CAPITALS

Nigeria
Ethiopia
Eritrea
Mali
Egypt
Senegal
Sierra Leone
Zimbabwe
Uganda
Sudan
Rwanda
Angola
Zambia
Somalia
Liberia
Kenya
Burkina Faso
Morocco
Libya
Namibia

GEOGRAPHICAL TERMS

Antipodes
Isthmus
Valley
Strait
Archipelago
Cape
Equator
Atoll
Peninsula
Tributary

FAMOUS SHIPS AND BOATS

Mary Rose
RMS *Titanic*
Hispaniola
Pequod
RMS *Lusitania*
Rainbow Warrior

RMS *Queen Elizabeth 2*
HMS *Victory*
Cutty Sark
Queen Anne's Revenge
Aurora
Mayflower
HMS *Beagle*
Kon-Tiki
Argo

MUPPETS
Kermit the Frog
Miss Piggy
Fozzie Bear
Scooter
Gonzo
Rowlf the Dog
Animal
Dr Julius Strangepork
Beaker
Statler and Waldorf

BOYS AND GIRLS

Male	Female
Buck	Doe
Jack	Jenny
Billy	Nanny
Boar	Sow
Cob	Pen

Drake	Duck
Peacock	Peahen
Ram	Ewe
Stallion	Mare

IVY LEAGUE
Brown University
Columbia University
Cornell University
Dartmouth College
Harvard University
Princeton University
University of Pennsylvania
Yale University

TEMPERATURE SCALES

°F	K
212	373
98.6	310
69.8	294
32	273

THE WORKS
OF OSCAR WILDE

Lady Windermere's Fan
A Woman of No Importance
Salomé
An Ideal Husband
The Importance of Being Earnest
The Picture of Dorian Gray
The Canterville Ghost

THE ORGANS
OF THE BODY

A Brain

B Lungs

C Heart

D Spleen

E Liver

F Stomach

G Kidneys

H Pancreas

I Intestines

J Urinary Bladder

THE HITS OF
MICHAEL JACKSON

'Ben'
'Don't Stop 'Til You Get
  Enough'
'Rock with You'

'One Day In Your Life'
'Beat It'
'Billie Jean'
'Say Say Say'
'Bad'
'I Just Can't Stop Loving You'
  (with Siedah Garrett)
'The Way You Make Me Feel'
'Dirty Diana'
'Man In The Mirror'
'Black Or White'
'Earth Song'
'You Are Not Alone'
'Blood On The Dance Floor'

COUNTRY CALLING
CODES

+61

+55

+33

+49

+91

+234

+7

+27

+44

+1

THE GREAT LAKES
Lake Superior
Lake Huron
Lake Michigan
Lake Erie
Lake Ontario

SANTA'S REINDEER
Dasher
Dancer
Prancer
Vixen
Comet
Cupid
Donner
Blitzen

CLUEDO
Suspects
Colonel Mustard
Miss Scarlett
Mrs Peacock
Mrs White
Professor Plum
Reverend Green

Rooms
Ballroom
Billiard Room
Conservatory
Dining Room
Hall
Kitchen
Library
Lounge
Study

Weapons
Candlestick
Dagger
Lead Pipe
Revolver
Rope
Wrench

INFAMOUS ASSASSINATIONS
Yitzhak Rabin
Abraham Lincoln
Julius Caesar
John Lennon
Mahatma Gandhi
Malcolm X
John F. Kennedy
Archduke Franz Ferdinand
Dr Martin Luther King, Jr
Robert F. Kennedy

FAMOUS EXPLORERS

Amerigo Vespucci

Marco Polo

Hernán Cortés

Abel Tasman

Christopher Columbus

James Cook

Admiral Zheng He

Sir Walter Raleigh

Ferdinand Magellan

David Livingstone

LONDON TUBE LINES

Victoria

Central

Circle

Hammersmith & City

Bakerloo

District

Metropolitan

Jubilee

Northern

Piccadilly

Waterloo & City

BACK IN THE USSR

State	Capital
Armenia	Yerevan
Azerbaijan	Baku
Byelorussian	Minsk
Estonia	Tallinn
Georgia	Tbilisi
Kazakhstan	Astana
Kyrgyzstan	Bishkek
Latvia	Riga
Lithuania	Vilnius
Moldova	Chişinău
Russia	Moscow
Tajikistan	Dushanbe
Turkmenistan	Ashgabat
Ukraine	Kyiv
Uzbekistan	Tashkent

THE HITS OF MADONNA

'Crazy For You'

'Justify My Love'

'Like A Prayer'

'Like A Virgin'

'Live To Tell'

'Music'

'Open Your Heart'

'Papa Don't Preach'

'Take A Bow'

'This Used To Be My Playground'

'Vogue'

'Who's That Girl'

THE TEN COMMANDMENTS

1 You shall have no other Gods before me.
2 You shall not make for yourself an idol.
3 You shall not make wrongful use of the name of the Lord your God.
4 Remember the Sabbath day and keep it holy.
5 Honour your father and your mother
6 You shall not murder.
7 You shall not commit adultery.
8 You shall not steal.
9 You shall not bear false witness against your neighbour.
10 You shall not covet your neighbour's house or belongings.

SO WHAT EXACTLY DO YOU DO?

Candle maker
Horse groom
Barrel maker
Bargeman
Writer
Curer of animal hides
Wagon maker
Cloth and dry goods dealer
Fruit and vegetable seller
Wig maker
Roofer

QUOTES FROM THE MOVIES

The Silence of the Lambs
Casablanca
On the Waterfront
Love Story
Gone with the Wind
The Wizard of Oz
Titanic
She Done Him Wrong
Wall Street
Dead Poets Society

NATIONAL FLAGS

A Bosnia and Herzegovina

B New Zealand

C Canada

D Portugal

E Ecuador

F Sri Lanka

G Malaysia

H India

I Saudi Arabia

J Lebanon

K Turkmenistan

L Cyprus

M Panama

N Brazil

O Zimbabwe

P Angola

Q Vanuatu

R Algeria

S Uruguay

T Kazakhstan

U Seychelles

V Albania

W Malta

X Croatia

Y Mongolia

JAZZ SOUBRIQUETS

Lady Day

Yardbird (or Bird)

Lockjaw

Duke

Jelly Roll

Django

Dizzy

Cannonball

Fats

Count

THE PLANET'S BIGGEST DESERTS

Sahara

Arabian

Gobi

Patagonian

Rub'al Khali

Great Victoria

Kalahari

Great Basin

Chihuahuan

Thar

THE BOROUGHS OF NEW YORK

The Bronx

Manhattan

Queens

Brooklyn

Staten Island

CITY NICKNAMES

New Orleans

Cairo

Oxford

Rome

Detroit

Venice

Las Vegas

New York

Beijing

Chicago

THE MOVIES OF STEVEN SPIELBERG

Jaws (1975)

Raiders of the Lost Ark (1981)

E.T. the Extra-Terrestrial (1982)

The Color Purple (1985)

Schindler's List (1993) (Winner)

Saving Private Ryan (1998)

Munich (2005)

THE CONTINENTS

North America

South America

Antarctica

Africa

Europe

Asia

Australia/Oceania

SOUTH AMERICAN CAPITALS

Buenos Aires

Brasília

Santiago

Bogotá

Quito

Georgetown

Asunción

Lima

Montevideo

Caracas

SACRED TEXTS

Sikhism

Jainism

Shinto

Hinduism

Christianity

Buddhism

Islam

Judaism

Taoism

STEVENSON'S TREASURE ISLAND

Jim Hawkins

Squire Trelawney

Captain Smollett

Long John Silver

Ben Gunn

Blind Pew

Captain Flint

Doctor Livesey

Billy Bones

FAMOUS COUPLES

Nefertiti

Lauren Bacall

Josephine

Elizabeth Barrett Browning

Courtney Love

Mumtaz Mahal

Yoko Ono

Grace Kelly

Delilah

Wallis Simpson

NOVELS OF JANE AUSTEN

Sense and Sensibility

Pride and Prejudice

Mansfield Park

Emma

Persuasion

Northanger Abbey

GREAT WORKS OF PHILOSOPHY

David Hume

Friedrich Nietzsche

Voltaire

Charles Darwin

Thomas Hobbes

Isaac Newton

René Descartes

Ludwig Wittgenstein

Thomas Aquinas

Karl Marx and Friedrich Engels

Immanuel Kant

Aristotle

Niccolò Machiavelli

Plato

Thomas More

SCIENTIFIC BREAKTHROUGHS

Tim Berners-Lee

Albert Einstein

William Harvey

Neils Bohr

Louis Pasteur

Isaac Newton

Charles Darwin

Sigmund Freud

Stephen Hawking

Nicolaus Copernicus

PARTS OF SPEECH

Verb

Noun

Adverb

Pronoun

Adjective

Preposition

Conjunction

Interjection

COMIC BOOK ALTER EGOS

Incredible Hulk

Captain Marvel

Ghost Rider

Robin

Wolverine

Superman

Spider-Man

Wonder Woman

Captain America

Batman

ORSON WELLES' FEATURE FILMS

Citizen Kane

The Magnificent Ambersons

The Stranger

The Lady from Shanghai

Macbeth

Othello

Mr. Arkadin

Touch of Evil

The Trial

Chimes at Midnight

The Immortal Story

F for Fake

PLATE TECTONICS

African Plate

Antarctic Plate

Arabian Plate

Australian Plate

Caribbean Plate

Cocos Plate

Eurasian Plate
Indian Plate
Juan de Fuca Plate
Nazca Plate
North American Plate
Pacific Plate
Philippine Plate
Scotia Plate
South American Plate

THE MUSICALS OF ANDREW LLOYD WEBBER

The Likes of Us (1965; first
  performed in 2005)
*Joseph and the Amazing
  Technicolor Dreamcoat* (1968)
Jesus Christ Superstar (1970;
  first performed in 1971)
Jeeves (1975; revived as *By Jeeves*)
Evita (1976)
Tell Me on a Sunday (1979)
Cats (1981)
Song and Dance (1982; including
  music from *Variations* and
  Tell Me on a Sunday)
Starlight Express (1984)
The Phantom of the Opera (1986)
Aspects of Love (1989)
Sunset Boulevard (1993)

Whistle Down the Wind (1996)
The Beautiful Game (2000;
  revived as *The Boys in the
  Photograph*)
The Woman in White (2004)
Phantom: Love Never Dies (2010)

WHO RECORDED THE ALBUM?

Frank Sinatra
John Coltrane
The Beach Boys
Aretha Franklin
Van Morrison
Neil Young
Black Sabbath
ABBA
Stevie Wonder
Kraftwerk
Bob Marley & The Wailers
Blondie
The Clash
The Police
Paul Simon
Prince
U2
Public Enemy
De La Soul
Red Hot Chili Peppers
REM

Blur
Alanis Morissette
Coldplay
The White Stripes

BRITISH PRIME MINISTERS

Sir Winston Churchill
(Conservative)
Clement Attlee (Labour)
Winston Churchill
(Conservative)
Sir Anthony Eden
(Conservative)
Harold Macmillan
(Conservative)
Sir Alec Douglas-Home
(Conservative)
Harold Wilson (Labour)
Edward Heath (Conservative)
Harold Wilson (Labour)
James Callaghan (Labour)
Margaret Thatcher
(Conservative)
John Major (Conservative)
Tony Blair (Labour)
Gordon Brown (Labour)

IN A GALAXY FAR, FAR AWAY...

The Phantom Menace
Attack of the Clones
Revenge of the Sith
A New Hope
The Empire Strikes Back
Return of the Jedi

FORMULA 1 CHAMPIONS

Michael Schumacher
Juan Manuel Fangio
Alain Prost
Jack Brabham
Jackie Stewart
Niki Lauda
Nelson Piquet
Ayrton Senna

LINES FROM SHAKESPEARE

Twelfth Night
Hamlet
Romeo and Juliet
King Henry IV, Part I
Merchant of Venice
Macbeth
Richard III

Julius Caesar
A Midsummer Night's Dream
The Taming of the Shrew

Eugene Cernan
Harrison Schmitt

WHO SAID WHAT? (PART II)

Nelson Mandela
Marilyn Monroe
Thomas Jefferson
Muhammad Ali
Oscar Wilde
Robert F. Kennedy
W. C. Fields
Confucius
G.K. Chesterton
Elizabeth I

WALKING ON THE MOON

Neil Armstrong
Edwin 'Buzz' Aldrin
Charles Conrad
Alan Bean
Alan Shepard
Edgar Mitchell
David Scott
James Irwin
John Young
Charles Duke

WILLY WONKA'S GOLDEN TICKET WINNERS

Charlie Bucket
Mike Teavee
Augustus Gloop
Veruca Salt
Violet Beauregarde

WORLD'S SMALLEST COUNTRIES

Malta
Maldives
Saint Kitts & Nevis
Marshall Islands
Liechtenstein
San Marino
Tuvalu
Nauru
Monaco
Vatican City

WARSAW PACT COUNTRIES

Albania

Bulgaria

Czechoslovakia

East Germany

Hungary

Poland

Romania

USSR

THE NOVELS OF ERNEST HEMINGWAY

The Torrents of Spring

The Sun Also Rises

A Farewell to Arms

To Have and Have Not

For Whom the Bell Tolls

Across the River and into the Trees

The Old Man and the Sea

Islands in the Stream

The Garden of Eden

Under Kilimanjaro/True at First Light

FRIENDS

Character / Actor

Chandler Bing / Matthew Perry

Phoebe Buffay / Lisa Kudrow

Monica Geller / Courteney Cox

Ross Geller / David Schwimmer

Rachel Greene / Jennifer Aniston

Joey Tribbiani / Matt LeBlanc

MULTIPLE 'TIME' PERSON OF THE YEAR

Franklin D. Roosevelt

Joseph Stalin

Winston Churchill

George Marshall

Harry S. Truman

Dwight D. Eisenhower

Lyndon B. Johnson

Richard Nixon

Ronald Reagan

Deng Xiaoping

Mikhail Gorbachev

Bill Clinton

George W. Bush

GENERIC PRODUCT NAMES

Biro

Sellotape (or Scotch Tape)

Frisbee

Velcro

Winnebago

Tupperware

Macintosh

Post-it Notes

Hoover

Jacuzzi

EGYPTIAN GODS AND GODDESSES

Amun

Ra

Atum

Osiris

Isis

Anubis

Horus

Nut

Anuket

Seth

ORIGINAL US COLONIES

Connecticut

Delaware

Georgia

Maryland

Massachusetts

New Hampshire

New Jersey

New York

North Carolina

Pennsylvania

Rhode Island

South Carolina

Virginia

STEPHEN SONDHEIM MUSICALS

A Funny Thing Happened on the Way to the Forum

A Little Night Music

Anyone Can Whistle

Assassins

Bounce (a.k.a. Road Show)

Company

Do I Hear a Waltz?

Follies

Gypsy

Into the Woods

Merrily We Roll Along

Pacific Overtures

Passion

Saturday Night

Sunday in the Park with George
Sweeney Todd
The Frogs
West Side Story

SCALES

pH Scale
Saffir/Simpson Scale
Fujita Scale
Apgar Scale
Glasgow Coma Scale
Mohs Scale
Kinsey Scale
Douglas Sea Scale
Richter Scale
Beaufort Scale

TOUR DE FRANCE WINNERS

Lance Armstrong (USA)
Jacques Anquetil (France)
Eddy Merckx (Belgium)
Bernard Hinault (France)
Miguel Indurain (Spain)
Philippe Thys (Belgium)
Louison Bobet (France)
Greg LeMond (USA)

HEART DIAGRAM

A   Superior Vena Cava
B   Right Atrium
C   Left Atrium
D   Right Ventricle
E   Left Ventricle
F   Inferior Vena Cava
G   Aorta
H   Pulmonary Artery
I   Papillary Muscles
J   Mitral Valve
K   Tricuspid Valve
L   Pulmonary Valve

PEACE TREATIES

Treaty of Verdun
Treaty of Ramla
Peace of Cateau-Cambrésis
Peace of Westphalia
Treaty of Utrecht
Treaty of Aix-la-Chapelle
Treaty of Nanjing
Treaty of Guadalupe Hidalgo
Treaty of Vereeniging
Treaty of Portsmouth
Comprehensive Test Ban Treaty
   (CTBT)

BOOK OF THE MOVIE

The Life and Opinions of
  Tristram Shandy, Gentleman
  (Laurence Sterne)
The Orchid Thief
  (Susan Orlean)
Heart of Darkness
  (Joseph Conrad)
Do Androids Dream of Electric
  Sheep? (Philip K. Dick)
Dangerous Liaisons (Pierre
  Choderlos de Laclos)
Inconceivable (Ben Elton)
Q&A (Vikas Swarup)
The Death and Life of
  Dith Pran (Sidney Schanberg)
Midwich Cuckoos
  (John Wyndam)
Romeo and Juliet
  (William Shakespeare)

SPACE SHUTTLE NAMES

Columbia
Challenger
Discovery
Atlantis
Endeavour

ART GALLERIES OF THE WORLD

Florence
Bruges
Saint Petersburg
Dublin
Los Angeles
New York
Paris
Madrid
Moscow
Washington, D.C.
London
Berlin

PLAGUES OF EGYPT

Water to blood
Frogs
Lice
Flies
Diseased livestock
Boils
Hail
Locusts
Darkness
Death of the firstborn

OPERAS

Wolfgang Amadeus Mozart
Ludwig van Beethoven

Gioacchino Rossini

Giuseppe Verdi

Johan Strauss II

Pyotr Tchaikovsky

Giacomo Puccini

Richard Strauss

Leoš Janáček

Kurt Weill

Benjamin Britten

Igor Stravinsky

FIRST LADIES

Bess Truman

Mamie Eisenhower

Jacqueline Kennedy-Onassis

Claudia 'Lady Bird' Johnson

Pat Nixon

Betty Ford

Rosalynn Carter

Nancy Reagan

Barbara Bush

Hillary Clinton

Laura Bush

Michelle Obama

NAUTICAL TERMS

Bow

Keel

Knot

League

Port

Rigging

Starboard

Plimsoll Line

Fathom

Galley

GOLD MEDAL OLYMPIANS

Michael Phelps

Larissa Latynina

Paavo Nurmi

Mark Spitz

Carl Lewis

Bjørn Dæhlie

Birgit Fischer-Schmidt

Sawao Kato

Jenny Thompson

Matt Biondi

Ray Ewry

SI UNITS

Metre

Kilogram

Second

Ampere

Kelvin

Candela

Mole

WRITE YOUR NOTES HERE

WRITE YOUR NOTES HERE

WRITE YOUR NOTES HERE